GROWN-ASS MAN

GROWN-ASS MAN
CEDRIC THE ENTERTAINER

BALLANTINE BOOKS ● NEW YORK

A Ballantine Book
Published by The Ballantine Publishing Group

Copyright © 2002 by Cedric "The Entertainer"

All rights reserved under International and Pan-American Copyright Conventions. Published in the United States by The Ballantine Publishing Group, a division of Random House, Inc., New York, and simultaneously in Canada by Random House of Canada Limited, Toronto.

Ballantine is a registered trademark and the Ballantine colophon is a trademark of Random House, Inc.

www.ballantinebooks.com

Library of Congress Cataloging-in-Publication Data is available upon request.

ISBN 0-345-44778-6

Manufactured in the United States of America

First Edition: January 2002

10   9   8   7   6

DEDICATION

To my mom, Rosetta; my wife, Lorna; my kids, Tiara and Croix;
my sister, Sharita K. Wilson, and family (Eric and Canaan);
my manager and partner, Eric C. Rhone (A Bird and a Bear,
baby!); and of course, to my fans.

TABLE OF CONTENTS

FOREWORD

Cedric the Intelligent Entertainer is what I like to call my top client and best friend of twenty years. While he personifies the ordinary guy who possesses an extraordinary ability to make people laugh and feel like family, Cedric is, in fact, an extraordinary guy whose talents happen to be equivalent.

His rare and unique blend of good sense, sound judgment, business acumen, natural comedic talent, creativity, versatility, and charisma has elevated him to the threshold of superstardom.

With his clean observational humor, Cedric allows his broad cross-cultural audience the opportunity to experience, commemorate, and reflect upon the funny and sometimes quirky good times in life. He keeps it simple, yet hilarious, with heartwarming stories anyone can relate to. Behind every joke Cedric has ever written or told, there is a point of personal reference which is one of the reasons people from all walks of life warm up to him and feel as if they have known him for years, like a close friend or relative.

Under the umbrella of laughter, his intelligence and creativity shine through, and I am constantly inspired by his appreciation of education, the arts, politics, and the global community, all of which he brings to his performances. Cedric shows his appreciation to his fans by giving back through the Cedric the Entertainer Charitable Foundation. This foundation is dedicated to providing moral and financial support for youths and families in need of assistance toward higher education, with scholarships as well as experiential education through domestic and foreign travel.

Hundreds of years from now when the time capsule is opened, I am certain that audiences from a new world will view excerpts from Cedric the Entertainer's career as some of the funniest commentary on everyday real-life experiences, and he will stand alone as the definitive blueprint for being a Grown-Ass Man in the twenty-first century.

—Eric C. Rhone

SPECIAL ACKNOWLEDGMENTS

To Karen Hunter, thank you for coming in and directing traffic on this piece. You did a wonderful job. Much appreciated. Also to Todd Gold, for your excellent input and guidance.

ACKNOWLEDGMENTS

To my family and friends, thank you for the love and support. To (Team Cedric): my #1 assistant, Kimberly Logan, who keeps my professional life tight; to Kelvin Bland, my tour manager, let's keep rolling, playa; to my publicist, Marla Winston, who makes sure everyone knows everything there is to know about this grown-ass man. To Andrea Nelson and all of the staff at Creative Artists Agency and my attorney Nina Shaw, thanks for the opportunities and for watching my back. And to Eric C. Rhone, I give you perpetual props.

To Jeremie Ruby-Strauss, my editor at Ballantine, nice working with you. Also to Anita Diggs, Gina Centrello, Nancy Miller, Peter Borland, Kim Hovey, and Michelle Aielli at Ballantine, and to Dan Strone at Trident Media Group. To my brother-in-law, Eric Wilson, and all of my St. Louis family from day one. Laff-A-Minute Prod., Darren Robinson, and the Truelove family. To Stan Lathan, my consigliere (I watch too much *Godfather*), thanks for everything.

To my dog, Steve Harvey, you my boy! And to the rest of the Kings of Comedy, my brothers in comedy—Bernie and D.L.

To Moncino North, my little Cousin Melvin Boyce aka Deep Red, Young "D" (You broke my heart.), Aunt Arlene,

Uncle Stanley, Eric Hubbard (my Uncle Big E), all my uncles, aunts, and cousins, and my people in Caruthersville, Missouri. To Rachel and my dad, Kittrell Kyles (big holla!).

I'd like to acknowledge the Funny Bone Comedy Club in St. Louis and all my peeps that used to kick it wit me at The Wiz in East St. Louis. To all of my homies on lockdown and knowing that is so real. To Nell and Perk (thanks for "Ced's Backyard"). To all the people that work at the Magic radio station in the STL.

To K.P. and Becky Parker. To Teri J. Vaughn aka Lovita . . . and all my *Steve Harvey Show* family.

To the Boogie Man and all my people from BET, and to Russell Simmons for giving us *Def Comedy Jam*. To my man, Bernie Brillstein, who gave me my first television deal. To Steve Smooke, my man Chris Flores, and the Moodswing Family. To all my people over at Bud Light.

To all of the black comedy clubs throughout the country. To all the comedians out there who are putting it down and still in the hustle. To Nelly and the St. Lunatics for representing the STL in a multi-platinum way. To all my brothers in the Kappa Alpha Psi fraternity.

To Terry Claybon, professional boxing coach. To Levine Hat Shop in St. Louis, no doubt! To Reggie J. Custom Clothing.

And to anybody I forgot: You know I love you like a play cuz'n! But you should have paged me so you could've gotten a shout out!

GROWN-ASS MAN

Growing up ain't easy, but it's a fact of life that every man must face. A lot of men think they're grown. But you ain't a grown-ass man just because you've reached the age of twenty-one. Being a grown man means you've earned your stripes through life experiences. You have developed a certain approach to life, as well as your own personal point of view. And it means you are able to take care of yourself and others.

I didn't realize I was a grown-ass man until I was well into my thirties. I was married, had a pre-teenaged daughter and a baby on the way. I had my own house, own car, and my entire family relied on me. When I suddenly realized that I was now the person that everyone counts on, the way I used to count on my daddy or lean hard on my mama, when it was my turn to be up at bat, that's when I realized I'm a grown-ass man. You see, that's when you start to open the door for women and stop letting your pants hang off your behind. You realize there ain't nothing cute about showing your underwear to the whole world.

First and foremost, a grown-ass man pays his bills. If you, as a thirty-year old, are still living in your mama's basement, asking her for twenty dollars to take your girlfriend to the movies, you are *not* a grown-ass man. In St. Louis we call them "basement niggas" because they live in the basement and think it's their own apartment, but they ain't paying not one bill or chipping in on food or nothing. But being in that basement—separate from the main house—gives them a sense of adulthood.

Now, just because a grown man pays the bills doesn't mean he loses his cool if they don't get paid quite on time. When you're just starting out, you may have a tendency to panic about paying the electricity, gas, cable, and credit cards the day after they come in. But when you become a grown-ass man, you acquire a whole different attitude. Bills come that don't scare you. It's when the bill collector wants to take things out or turn things off that you start paying attention.

But with bills, you know nothing's going to happen if you don't pay them right away. After the bill, they may send you a second notice, a kind of how-you-doing card. Then comes a third notice. And the bills turn colors when it gets closer to the turn-off or take-out point. It goes from white to red, then finally it gets to the handwritten note that says, "Dawg, don't make me come over there." That's when you pay.

Of course before a grown-ass man pays that one, he might send it back with a little note saying, "Come on, partna. I'm waiting. It is whatever!"

When you become the head of your situation and you take responsibility for that situation, it takes up a lot of your energy. Since you can't sit back and get comfortable having your mama or your woman take care of you anymore, you have to try to conserve your energy. When my 16-year-old cousin asks me to play full-court basketball, I've got to say, "No thanks, dawg!" Because

I know I'll hurt my whole left side trying to run up and down the court. And I got shit to do tomorrow.

Take Billy Dee Williams. He never ran in any of his films. Or think about Barry White. He never ever moved onstage. Barry sweated like a new inmate, but he never moved. And Snoop Doggy Dogg, well, y'all know Snoop Dogg's problem. . . .

This grown-ass man thing ain't new. I ain't the first to think of it. God was the original G-A-M . . . grown-ass man. He set the example. He was cool. He didn't expend too much energy. On the seventh day, he didn't go out and create something else. He didn't go out and play golf. He didn't barbecue. He didn't go to his mama's house and fix the screen door. The Man kicked back in front of the big screen—that's the world—and chilled. On the seventh day, he rested.

I've got some friends who don't understand this principle. They call me up and say, "Ced, you want to go for a hike?"

A hike?

I say, "I ain't got time to be hiking. I'm chilling. Besides, I got on church shoes."

"Cedric, I'm riding my bike from Utah to Oregon," they say. "You want to come along?"

I'm suspicious. But I reply, "Hell naw!"

"I'm not riding a bike across three states. Look, partna, I'm a grown-ass man. That's why I got a *driver's license!*"

Then they have the nerve to ask if I want to sponsor them, talking about getting fifty cents a mile.

They ask, "So can I sign you up, Ced?"

"How far you going?"

"Twenty-two hundred miles."

Brother's smiling.

Now I know why he quit his job, because he's going to make more riding his bike than he did working.

"What're you going to do with that money?" I ask.

"I'm helping cure cancer."

That's when I give him that look. And then I wait. I know my friends don't ride bikes—not for real for real. Finally brother cracks.

"Okay, I might also move out of my mama's basement and put a down payment on a car so I don't have to ride my bike anymore."

I don't do little things like I used to. I stand up slower. I go to sleep slower. And I make love . . . well, I used to do it all night, but now it takes me all night to do it. I want to wait until *The Sopranos* are over. These days, my version of foreplay is: "Baby, I'll play with you 'fore my show starts—after that, I'm busy."

I no longer want incredible, mind-blowing, forget-about-all-your-past-lovers, Prince-doesn't-even-do-it-like-this sex. I simply want some sex. According to all the magazines, the goal used to be a multi-orgasm. Then it was the two-hour orgasm. Then it was the tantric orgasm lasting for a whole day. A whole day, dawg?! Just give me one good one and I'm solid. I'm back to the playoffs.

There are other little things that come with the territory, too. Like you don't want to use silly-ass nicknames anymore. Now, old school is one thing. Like I knew an old guy, Shoe Box Wilson. He was so poor he couldn't afford shoes—he just wore the boxes. He told me he wore some of the best of them too—Johnston and Murphy, Stacy Adams. Or this friend of mine, Charcoal Taylor. Dark brother, Charcoal was. He was behind-the-refrigerator dark. Under-the-bed black. If he were to lie in the street, you'd swear he was a speed bump. That's how dark he was. Then there was Una Johnson. Una was short for unattractive. But now you hear us on the radio doing shout outs:

"I want to give it up to Lil' Stomach Ache, Lil' Carpet Burn, Lil' Pistol Whip, my boy Lil' Leprechaun . . ."

I met this brother named Darryl. He said to me, "But you can call me Delicious."

What, playa?! What you say?! Come again?!

I said, "Listen dawg, I'm a grown-ass man, and I'm not calling another dude 'Delicious'!"

What if he's way down the street? I'm supposed to be yelling, "Yo, Delicious! Wait up."?!

I don't think so. I'm a grown-ass man!

GROWN-ASS MAN

PART I

THE MAKING OF A GROWN-ASS MAN

CHAPTER ONE

HEAVEN HELP US!

Church was a big part of my growing up. Back then, it seemed like church was so important. It was about community. It was a time when everybody got together. Sunday was the day for the whole family. You'd go home, have dinner together—cousins and uncles would show up, and it'd be a nice day. It was like the movie *Soul Food.*

That's how it was in Caruthersville, Missouri, where I lived until age ten. It was the kind of small town where the lady across the street could whip your butt if she saw you doing something wrong and your mama wasn't home. I couldn't walk home from school without hearing her.

"Cedric, get off that man's grass! You know that man don't want nobody on his grass!"

That was Miss Tessie Mae.

"I hate her," I'd say under my breath.

"I heard you!" she'd yell.

And that lady really did hear you even though she was sitting way up on her porch. She would whip your ass and then make sure you got another whipping when your mama got home from work. Those were the good old days.

You can imagine how important Sunday was in a town like that. My grandmother was one of those real religious people who believed the Lord did everything. She was constantly muttering something about the Lord.

"Ooooh, I woke up this morning, and the Lord put on my house shoes, yes he did. Then I was drivin' down the street and the light turned red, but the Lord told me to keep on going."

"No he didn't, Grandma," I said. "The Lord doesn't tell people to break the law."

I'd hear her speech every Sunday morning for years to come. She didn't care what time you got home from partying on Saturday night. She didn't care that you were sound asleep—one of those good, satisfying, deep sleeps. She'd come in and hit you with the speech.

"You can't tell me you've got time to party on Saturday, but you ain't got time for the Lord on Sunday. Get on up and go on in there." And you'd know it was useless to argue.

Then you'd find yourself sitting up at church with your night-club clothes on, trying to stay awake. And you aren't the only one. Everybody's nodding—except your grandma and mother. They see your head start jerking like a fishing lure, your eyelids dropping, and you know what happens next? You get that pinch.

"Ouch!"

Then you look the other way.

"Man, you got a peppermint, a Certs, a lemon drop, or something? I'm trying to tell you, I ain't gonna make it."

But that was back in the day, before Altoids. Because two or more Altoids will freeze your whole head.

Back then, when you're ten, you're still trying to resist. You start thinking about your daddy. He never goes to church. You see him sitting at home, watching television, drinking a beer, scratching himself, having the kind of good old time you wish you could have.

In fact, he'd never look as happy as he did while waving good-bye and talking about praying for him.

"Y'all pray for me now," he'd say. "Go on ahead."

So you'd turn to your grandma.

"What about Daddy?"

"What about him?" she'd reply.

"He don't never go to church?"

"Your daddy knows better. But he's decided he'd rather be going to hell."

And you know she's right. You know your daddy's in trouble. You picture yourself arriving at the pearly gates and St. Peter's saying to him, "Hey dawg, remember that Sunday you didn't feel like getting dressed?"

That's when I think, "A little church might be good for me. Let me just run down and get a TiVo so I don't miss the game."

My favorite part about going to church was the change I got from my mother. It was just a few coins. I'd hit the bottom of the basket as I pretended to put the money in, making the basket jingle.

I wanted my mom to think I'd put the money in, though secretly I put it in my pocket. Only me and God knew. Then after church, I'd buy gum and suckers. I was fine until bedtime. Then I'd think, "Am I going to hell now?"

The other big thing to do on Sundays was go to the Dairy Queen, and everyone in church started to think about that around the same time. So about fifteen minutes before church was over, people started whispering to each other.

There'd be light bickering in which you could tell people were saying, "You go."

"No, you go."

"Just get up, I'm right behind you."

"That's right, amen . . . I went first *last* week!"

Then people made their moves. One person would pretend to cough and finally get up. He'd be followed by another. Next thing you know, everyone's at the Dairy Queen. The preacher, though not finished with his sermon, knew what was going on, and as the last person hurried out, he worked it right into his sermon, saying, "God wants you to . . . order me a Dilly bar."

"Amen," someone would say from the choir. "Make that two."

The Dairy Queen was right next door to the city jail, so often times you had relatives at the window, hollering down, "Hey, kinfolk, throw me up a banana split or a Blizzard or something."

"Naw, that's too messy. How about a Dilly bar?"

At least you got some visiting time in from the Dairy Queen.

That's how it was back in the day. But there seems to be less of that now. Society as a whole seems to be going in a totally different direction. Today, it doesn't seem like church and Sundays have the same importance. You have so many religious leaders, so many televangelists, who are as big as rappers. They're just as famous as the celebrities. They live inside their fame. These guys got private jets. They have mansions. They have money. They're living the same lifestyle as the celebrities. They're friends with Will Smith and Chris Tucker. They want them coming to their church—not so much to save them, but to be associated with them.

Church has become trendy. Choirs have record deals. Going to church nowadays is like going to a concert. It's semicool to go. It's star-studded, people looking around to see who's coming. If you're a celebrity, you get to park in a special parking lot and go in a special back door. You're a celebrity, you don't have to do the regular thing.

That's church in L.A. As if God cares that you're a celebrity, like there's going to be some special roped-off section in Heaven.

I go to church and folks got their instant box cameras with them. People wanting a picture and an autograph . . . during services.

"Can you sign this?"

"Uh, that's your Bible, dawg!"

"Yeah, sign right in Matthew, chapter 7 between verses 20 and 21."

I guess all of that has me a little tainted. The regular common folks want autographs. Is that necessary on a day when everyone should be normal? How do you get celebrity status in a church?

There's something about church and the church environment that indicates we all should be equal, because we're all looking for the same thing—salvation.

No matter what, you still have to go to church. When you

haven't been to church in a while, you start feeling guilty. You start having thoughts, like maybe the end is near, and suddenly you start hearing a deep, authoritative voice.

"You might want to get up in there, dawg."

"Is that you God?" you ask.

"I ain't saying. Alls I'm sayin' is you might want to get your behind into My house soon."

"What do you mean, soon?"

"I mean right now. Not now, but right now!"

Then you start promising yourself that you're going, but you don't make it.

"I'm gonna get on up 'n go on in," you say. "That's what I'm gonna do."

But you don't go, and the next week you raise the ante.

"I'm a go in and pray some, that's what I'm gonna do. I'm a iron my clothes on Saturday. That way, I can just hop right up and go on in."

It's easy to spot the brothers who haven't been to church for a long time. They're the ones who don't know what to do. They walk in thinking they're in a club and find themselves in the pulpit.

"Hey, player, these seats taken? These two?" pointing to the choir director's and deacon's seats. "Ah, they're somebody's seats? All right, damn!"

But he stays cool. He tries another seat.

"Hey, dawg, that's where the preacher sits. You can't sit there. That's where the preacher go!"

It's frightening when you do finally go to church after not having been in a long time. First, you might be identified as a visitor, which means you might have to stand up and have words. And that's a lot of pressure at a black church.

You don't know that church language, which is painfully obvious if you've got to follow that lady who's out traveling. She knows the whole little speech and everything. She gets up right in front of you, giving honor to God, looking you right in the eye.

"Pastor, members, and friends. I come to you on behalf of the Greenway Missionary Baptist Church, Greenway, Mississippi, where my reverend, the Honorable Thesselonious Archinkaid Junior the Third says . . ."

The brother behind her starts panicking. He's next. He starts talking to himself.

"I'm in trouble. I don't know none of that shit. What am I supposed to say?! I don't know none of what that woman's saying. All I know is hip-hop language."

Then he just thinks, "What the hell!" because when his turn comes, he stands up in the middle of the church and gives it a try.

"Ummm, ummm, first of all, givin' big ups to God, Reverend, you 'bout it, you 'bout it. Everybody, big ups. And the choir. Y'all real tight. Real tight. That's on everything. Big ups to y'all."

He keeps on rolling until the sister in the pew next to him leans over and whispers, "Sit your ass down."

The other pressure you might have to deal with going to church after a long dry spell is a good sermon. A good sermon puts a lot of damn pressure on you, boy. You're sitting in your seat and the preacher is doing his thing, calling people up. When he gets like that, he'll eventually find you. You'll think he's finished, but then the Lord will remind him you're there.

"Well, I feel it's just one more person in here that wants to come to the Lord," and he's looking directly at you.

A good sermon is dangerous. It gets you thinking. It starts that internal debate the preacher spoke about. You're in your seat going through it, thinking about it, telling yourself, "Damn, I should go on up there to the altar. I should go ahead on. Pastor's right. I should get my life together. Start right now. Today. If only I didn't . . . have that last little bit of weed left at the crib . . . I'm a join next week. That's what I'm gonna do."

Once, I went to an all-white Catholic church, and I noticed that they prayed differently than black folks. It's true. White folks be praying about trees, clean oceans, peace. They don't care what it is, as long as they're in church they're happy to pray.

"Oh Father, thank you for the trees. Thank you for the birds that fly, Father, and the rivers that run. And the streets we drive on. Amen."

Now you know, if you was at the Great Amount Give A Lot Missionary Baptist Church—in other words, a black church—the prayer is going to be totally different. Black folk pray for stuff that they need—like their lottery numbers to come through.

Then there's always that brother who comes out and prays the same way every time, and for the same things, and you know it's going to be long. You've been planning your escape. You saw

Heaven, and it looked like the open highway straight to home. Suddenly you're like, "Oh no, not him! Damn, the game's on!"

But that brother don't care about no game. He's got a whole list of praying to do.

"Dear Lord, you gave me government cheese. Yes you did, Father. I was able to make me a grilled cheese sandwich that was burnt around the edges just like I like it. And Father, when my cable got turned off, your kindness let me run cable from next door. Jesus, y'alright, you such a friend to me. In Jesus' name, Amen."

White folks are so orderly and solemn when they take communion. They're full of quiet contemplation. It ain't that way in a black church. There's always that brother sitting up all important, having the communion wine like he was at a club. He knocks one back and says, "Yo, usher, let me get two more of them. Y'all got any snacks? What's up playa, you gonna eat your cracker? Don't shush me, I'm just askin' if you was gonna eat your cracker?! I was just askin' . . . damn!"

CHAPTER TWO

MY MAMA KNOWS BEST

When I was around eleven, my family moved to Berkeley, Missouri, a suburb north of St. Louis. At the time, all the black families were moving from the inner city into the suburbs, and we didn't want to be left behind. Actually, we had to get out. White people were moving into the city, building lofts, decorating them with ferns, and ruining perfectly good ghettos.

My mother and father were divorced. My dad was pretty much a weekend dad.

For the most part growing up, I lived with my mama, my sister, and my grandmother. Being around all those women is where I started learning about things. I mean the real deal. I'm talking about all those little secrets that explain so much.

My grandmother used to have this bag hanging over the bathtub. I had no idea what it was, so I used to fill it with water and play army man in the tub, squirting water all over the damn place.

My mother busted me doing that and gave me a whooping.

"What did I do?"

"You touched that!" my mother said, pointing to what had been my rifle.

"What is it?"

She explained what it was and what it was used for, and . . .

"Ewwwwwwwwwwwwwwwwwwwwwwwww! I ain't never gonna do that again."

I learned more than I needed to know. I remember asking, "What's going on with Grandma? It's snowing outside and she's fanning herself, saying it's hotter 'n hell."

"That's the change," my mother said.

"And, Mama, sometimes Grandma's nice, and then sometimes she's . . ."

"That's the change, too, baby."

"The change?!"

"Menopause."

"What's that?"

She explained and told me it was happening with Grandma, and I said—

"Ewwwwwwwwwwwwww!"

Forget what my grandma was going through. My sister changed right before my eyes. One day she was my sister. The next day she had breasts. Soon she was having lots of private conversations with my mother, and I was beginning to feel left out.

"What y'all talking about?"

"Nothing you need to know," my mother said.

That meant I absolutely had to know. I put my ear to the door and was shocked. It turned out my mother was telling my sister what it meant to be a woman and how to act like a lady.

Suddenly I was like, "Oh, I see how it is." That's when I found out about that box under the sink. I thought, "Hey, you know what? She was right, that was nothing I needed to know."

Growing up, my mother, Rosetta, was my hero. She seemed to have all of the answers. When I was little, I thought she had special powers. I thought my mother could stop anything that bled with a little bit of her spit. I would fall off my bike, skin up my arm and knee, come home with third-degree abrasions and bruises, and my mother always did the same thing. She took a napkin, wet it with a little bit of her spit, and rubbed my cuts.

"How's that, baby?"

"Mama, I need a skin graft, not just spit!"

"Okay, come here. Let me see it," she would say. "Oh, it's not that bad."

It didn't matter if my finger was cut off or if I broke my hand, she would wet a napkin and rub it on the affected area like everything was all right. And most of the times it was. My mother had a way of making everything all right.

She is a very pretty lady. She used to remind me of Gladys Knight. You remember Gladys when she was still with the Pips. My mother had so much style. So much grace. And she was strong.

She raised my sister and me practically by herself. I know

there was a time when we were a family, when we lived with my father. I know because there are pictures of us, and we looked like a real family. But I don't remember any of that. We left when I was young, and I'm sure my sister, who is three years younger, can't remember either.

After leaving my father, my mother went back to school. She got her degree and didn't stop there. She went ahead and got her master's, too. She was a real determined person who never let any obstacle stop her.

In our neighborhood, everybody thought we were rich. That was my mother, again. Not only did she dress with style, she made sure my sister and I were sharp, too. Hell, I had matching baby clothes. I was matching before it was popular. I think Garanimals owes my mother some money, because they definitely stole my style. The kids would say, "Y'all rich!"

"I ain't rich, I had grilled cheese for dinner," I'd say.

My mother did have rich ideas and a rich way of thinking, though. She knew education was important. When she graduated, she became a teacher. She taught reading to elementary school kids in St. Louis.

While my mother was in school, we lived with my grandmother in a small four-bedroom house. It had a gas-burning stove in the middle of the house that served as the radiator. The kitchen was real small, too. After a year or so, my mother had an extra room built onto the house. That was the talk of the town. All the kids were so intrigued by this.

And when it was done, it was like new money. That room—which ended up being my mother's bedroom—had new paneling and air-conditioning. My grandmother didn't believe in air-conditioning. She liked the fan (she was old school). So we would all pile up in my mother's room and stay cool.

We had status items, like a microwave, when they were just coming into fashion. We had a toaster oven, too. We had things with remote controls and LED readouts. Stuff that made everyone pea green with envy.

"Man, you got a digital clock?" kids would ask.

"Yup."

"Cool."

It was like that then, remember? Simple things like a digital clock could attract hundreds.

"Can we watch the numbers change?"

"Maybe later."

As I got older, though, I became street savvy. I was able to bring home some goods for myself without spending a lot of money. The first thing I brought home was a clock radio. Then I got a television for my bedroom, and that caught my mother's attention.

"Cedric, are you stealing?"

"No, ma'am." *Kids today don't say that no more.*

My bedroom was four walls and a storeful of electronic equipment. My mom got worried when I added a VCR.

"Where'd you get that?"

"At the barbershop, ma."

Now, to understand the barbershop, you've got to understand the hookup.

You know black people are always looking for the hookup—

always looking to get something extra when we pay good money for something.

We have had to make do and get by for so long that we understand the value of a hookup. We've bought stuff from folks coming by the house selling boosted clothes—selling Polo and Fubu. We appreciate the bargain and the negotiation.

"Yo, I'm going to get the jeans, dawg, but I need you to throw in the shirt or something!"

We feel that if we're spending something, you got to give us something. Anytime we got to break off a little bit of cash, you need to show that you appreciate that. I think that's right. Especially when you consider what shit costs to make. Nikes cost like sixty-four cents to make in one of those third-world countries, and they want to charge $150 for a pair of sneakers. I think it's only right to throw something in with that purchase. Yeah, give me a hat, sweatband, shirt—something!

The hookup is dead serious. It's not something we hope to get—it's something we *gots* to get. But sometimes we take it a bit too far.

A brother'll walk into a burger joint and order a cheeseburger and turn around and say, "And can you hook me up with some fries?"

Now if the guy behind the counter hooked everybody up with fries, he'd get fired. But folks don't care.

"What do you mean I have to pay for the fries?" he'll say. "Why you can't just hook me up? I can't get a small fry?! It's not like I'm asking for a large! Damn, dude, just throw a handful of fries in my bag, then!"

In KFC, a brother'll order a two-piece and want to get hooked up on an extra wing. That's why those value meals became so very important to us. Somebody got real clever over at KFC. They figured it out. We love the hookup, so they included everything and gave it one price. So you get your two-piece, and they throw in the fries and drink for "free." That's shit we used to have to negotiate for.

You even have the hookup at the movies.

"Man, I'm willing to pay for my seat, but can you hook me up on the popcorn?"

Same thing with buying a car.

"I'll pay that much, but bro, you got to hook me up with the floor mats."

Even on a date:

"I'm going to buy you dinner; that's no prob. But babe, you're going to have to hook me up later on, if you know what I mean."

The ultimate hookup is at Price Club. It's one of those places where you can buy stuff in bulk for cheap prices. You can buy a jar of mayonnaise that can last like five years. I used to go there all the time—for the hookup. Every day, they would have these little stations set up with samples of food they're selling in the store to entice you to buy. One place you can sample some lasagna, another place in the store they are making sausages, another spot you can grab something to drink and maybe a slice of pie or cake. They really messed up with that. I would go there every Saturday for brunch. I wouldn't buy a damn thing. I would just go around to every single sample station and eat all day, like I was at a buffet or something.

The hookup has become so serious that I can see folks trying to get over on Judgment Day. Picture it: the line to the pearly gates is long, and everybody's wondering why it ain't moving. What's with the holdup? It was going smoothly, and then suddenly it jammed up. Everybody's looking around asking, "What's going on?"

You know what's going on? There's a brother up in the front asking, "Hey man, is Moses here? Tell him it's Dwayne. I just want to holler at him for a minute.

"He's busy? Oh, all right, I see my partna, Jesus. Yo, Jesus! Hook me up, man! You can't? Oh c'mon, man! Go around back and you'll hook me up? Okay, cool." *Ain't no back door to Heaven, y'all.*

So the barbershop was the place in the hood you'd go to get hooked up.

"Cedric, you mean to tell me you bought a VCR—at the barbershop?" my mother asked.

"Yeah, Mama. See, you spending way too much money on the things you want."

I also got a love seat for my room. You could get everything you needed at the barbershop—plus a haircut.

Growing up, I was responsible for doing most of the manly chores around the house, like taking out the garbage. If I didn't do something, my mother always had a way of finding out without even looking. It was like she had radar on me. She just knew. But one chore I never missed was on Saturdays, when I would wash the car.

We had one of the baddest cars in the neighborhood. My mother got a Monte Carlo, and it was the first year they made them with swivel seats. That was cool. I'd bring all my friends over and open the car door like I was David Copperfield at the start of a magic trick. My friends saw the car seats and were like, "So?" Then I'd hit the lever, swivel it out, and they'd go, "Ouuuuuuu." We were the toast of the neighborhood, my friend. So I was going to get the Monte Carlo washed—that was the only time I got to spend some real quality time with the car, because my mother wouldn't let me drive it. I was just going to get it washed, but once it was clean I felt it was necessary to take it for a spin around the hood. You know, show off a little. The brothers had seen the seats swivel. Now they could see how cool I looked driving the car.

So I went cruising. I stopped at the gas station to fill it up and ended up running into the pole at the station, banging the front fender. It should just be understood that any kid who goes for a joyride in his or her parent's car is going to ding it—or worse. It's guaranteed.

The fender got pretty beat up. Did I tell my mother what happened? No! In fact, I tried to turn that situation completely around. When she asked me about it, I became concerned and acted like I didn't know what happened.

"You know what? I don't know what happened to this car. I don't see nothing wrong to begin with. So if you see something wrong with it, whatever it is you see, I didn't have nothing to do with it."

There was a problem, though. There always is in a situation like that, right? The guy at the gas station called my mother because they had to replace the pole that I hit. She confronted me.

"Pole? They said I hit a pole? Now they need a new one?"

"That's what they said," she answered.

"Okay, well, even though they're lying, it's cool."

"It's cool?!" she said. "What you mean it's cool?! What are you going to do about that pole?!"

"Let me see if they got one at the barbershop. I need my hair cut anyway."

CHAPTER THREE

GET YOUR FREAK ON

The first time I ever got "romantic," you know, got busy with a girl, I got busted—by my sister.

At the time, my mother only knew that I was kinda into girls. She would see me being into them, talking on the corner, thrilling them with a bashful sensitivity that many of the mothers in the hood said reminded them of an adolescent Billy Dee Williams.

I was about sixteen years old. But my own mother couldn't see me as anything but her little boy. She didn't notice the change. My sister got boobs, but I got something more subtle— a devilish gleam in my eye.

I brought home a neighborhood girl, and I was trying to get my freak on. I didn't quite know what I was doing, but I was trying pretty damn hard to figure it out. Wanting a private place, we'd snuck into the garage and settled into the place where my sister and I kept our bicycles. We were kissing and rolling around and stuff when my sister walked in, looked right at us, and let out a surprised, high-pitched screech. She was louder than a car alarm going off. Talk about ruining the mood.

"Ouuuuuuuuuuuuuuuuuuuuu!"

I tried to tell her to wait, but she was gone so quickly. The last thing I heard was that siren of a voice of hers trailing off as she said, "I'm gonna tell Mama!"

And she did. She told my mother everything.

"Cedric, you know what he was doin'?! He was . . . ouuuuuuuuuu!"

That's when my mom realized I was into girls, and she started referring to me as "mannish."

"He's mannish," she would say. "He's a mannish little boy."

Mannish is like being Amish with a loaded gun. "Obadiah, unhand the girl and step away from the barn . . ."

My mother didn't quite know what to do when she found out that I'd become "mannish." She knew about Grandma's change. She could handle my sister becoming a woman. But she didn't know how to approach me becoming mannish. She made several attempts to talk to me about it, but she gave up and called my dad, who, being only a weekend father, didn't have much to say.

"Hey, um, boy," he said, "I heard about you and that girl. What'd you think you were doing?"

"Huh?" I'd learned it was always good to play dumb.

"In the garage . . . with that girl?"

Okay, I was caught. Change of tactics.

"Well, I'm a grown-ass man now."

"The hell you are!"

Of course, he was right.

I finally got the sex speech from my mother, which boiled down to two things: (1) being respectful to her house and (2) not having babies.

"You don't want to bring any kids home," she said. "You're a child yourself."

Like most sex talks at that time, though, there weren't any how-tos or what-not-to-dos. It wasn't like it is nowadays when kids actually get the talk in school. It's part of the curriculum. Where in the sixth grade, the teacher brings in a cucumber and a condom. I don't even want to think about how kids study for that test.

"Did you study for your sex test?"

"Not yet, mom. I'm going over to Vanessa's tonight and we're going to study together."

"Okay, don't forget your condoms."

Like I said, I had none of that, so whatever I did was mostly improvisation.

"Oops, sorry about that, baby. Let me try it over there."

Or else it was based on instructional material I'd read about in magazines like *Playboy*.

You know a guy can never admit it's his first time no matter what. It's always got to be this macho thing, even when you don't know what the hell you're doing. But how was I supposed to figure out what I was doing when I kept getting caught?

The next time, I was seventeen, and I had another neighborhood girl over. We were serious enough to be in the house rather than the garage. We were really getting into each other—shit was getting unbuttoned and unzipped—when I heard my mother drive up.

Suddenly, the eyes we were making at each other changed from looks of passion to looks that said, "Uh-oh!"

We'd barely gotten ourselves all zipped and buttoned back up when my mother was at the door. Both of us dove onto the sofa in the TV room. Luckily, we didn't collide midair. When my mother stepped into the room, we were gasping for air, sweating, confused, basically caught with our hands in the cookie jar, but still trying to play it off, playing it cool. Between breaths, I even managed to say, "Oh, hi . . . I didn't hear you come in."

But this was my mama. She knew. Mothers have a sixth sense that tells them what's going on with their babies. They can be across town and they get that telepathic *ping* that lets them know.

My mom played it cool, though. She walked through the room with a smile, but out of the corner of her eye she saw my pants were on backward. She kept walking until she got to the door, and then she looked back and said, "Come here."

"What?" I asked defensively. "We were just watching TV."

I was still halfway breathing hard.

"Why are you so out of breath?" she asked.

"Switching channels. That's all. I went through a lot of channels real fast."

"Come here."

I looked back and gave the girl a look that told her to keep the fire burnin', it'd be all right. Then I followed my mother.

She took me in the back and gave me the sex speech again. I was okay with the part of her talk about being respectful to the house. No problem, I'd respect the house. But then my mom said she wanted to talk to the girl, and that was it for me.

I was her son, so I could take whatever she needed to say. I'd heard the talk. I knew how to deal with her. But that poor girl had to get talked to about her morals from *my* mother? Embarrassing!

I heard the first part that went, "Young lady, I don't care if he is my son, you should not be over at a guy's house," and so on and so forth, and then I died.

Actually, I'm surprised I wasn't so traumatized that I was never able to ever try and have sex again. Imagine if I said to a girl, "We can only do it at my house if you promise to respect the house." Pause. "You do? Good. And there's one more thing. After we do it, my mom has to talk to you."

CHAPTER FOUR

MUSIC LESSONS

When I was growing up, there were about three songs, tops, with curse words in them. We got an exemption from punishment for saying one of those words because it was in a song. We got a cuss-for-free pass.

Nowadays, the problem is that nearly every song's got a cuss word in it. Even the love songs have them. So I feel sorry for kids today—the fun and excitement has been taken out of saying those words.

But try to imagine the sheer joy I had at seven years old when "Bad, Bad Leroy Brown" came on the radio.

"Bad, Bad Leroy Brown . . . baddest man in the whole *damn* town!"

To be able to say *damn* in front of my mother was so exciting. And I was on top of that line. I could be sound asleep in bed with my mom listening to the radio softly in her bedroom, and if that song came on, I was on top of the *damn*.

I sang that line with so much enthusiasm that my mother

would look at me and I'd say, "It's in the song, Mama. That's not me. It's in the *song*. I'm just singing what the song is singing."

The classic song, the one I looked forward to hearing on the radio most of all, was the Isley Brothers' "Fight the Power." That had the strongest curse word of all time.

". . . And when I roll with the punches/I got knocked on the ground/by all that *bullshit* going down . . ."

Boy, we'd wait on Ron Isley to get to the part where he'd say "bullshit," and then we'd sing it strong. Every kid in the hood sang it at the same time. It'd be nighttime, all the kids would be doing their homework, the radio on in the background, and then all of a sudden you'd hear the word *bullshit* from every home and apartment with a kid. It was like an epidemic of Tourette's, but you knew it was just the Isley Brothers on the radio.

The 1970s were a time when you heard a lot of great music: dance, funk, disco. There were bands—I mean brothers that actually played instruments—like Earth, Wind & Fire and Funkadelic. And there was stereo equipment—real stereo equipment.

This was the era of the big-ass record player. We had one with an arm that would pick the record up and drop it off. Before you got to hear any music, that arm had shit to do. They don't make record players like that any more. That was a serious piece of furniture. It wasn't just a stereo, there was a television in there, too. Then you flipped one side over and there was a checkerboard; the other side had a flower bed and a casket with Uncle Ellis in it. It was that big.

I had to dust it every Saturday. I could only dust it, I wasn't allowed to touch it. That shit cost money. If I tried to turn it on, just made a move like I was thinking about turning it on, my mother turned into Shaft: "Back off, Jack. Do you know how much that costs?"

But it was the kind of thing that made my friends think I was cool. They just had to look at it, know it was there and that it was mine.

"Ouuuuuuuu, man. That stereo is cool."

I'd grin like I was a twelve-year-old with his own Corvette.

Around that time, I went to some cool parties at the community center, and they all started out with the same tension. The girls were on one side of the room, and the guys would be on the other side. Everybody would be talking to friends, acting casual, like they had nothing else to do.

But you've never seen so many people with perfect vision out of the littlest corner of their eye. Everyone was waiting . . . and waiting . . .

It just took one cool guy to get everyone to mix. When *the* song came on, there would be that brother who walked up to a girl and said, "You wanna dance?" If he wasn't shot down, it was on. Then the rest of us were free to walk over there, too.

If he got turned down, it was another thirty or forty minutes before anybody got up the nerve to try again.

Once the dance got going, though, it was like being on *Soul Train*. Of course, everybody was really waiting on the slow dance. I don't know why they even call it a dance. It was more like a slow stand. You just stood and pressed together. There would be so much heat in the room that the teachers would be drawn in, and they would be slow dancing with each other.

Later on, I used to hang around with the deejay at our high school. He was a friend of mine. Actually, I don't know if he was really a friend, but he let me carry his equipment and that got me into the parties for free. That's another version of the hookup.

Going to all of those parties really got me into music. I listened to everything and began paying attention to artists like Frankie Beverly and Maze, David Sanborn, Jeffery Osborne. Luther. Big Luther, not Little Luther. I don't do the Little Luther. I like the Big, curl-ain't-quite-right Luther. That boy made all that money and his curl never curled all the way over. That was just something that always concerned me.

And I liked Teddy P. Teddy said something when he sang. He told you how to be a player. His songs were instructional.

"Turn off the lights . . . light a candle."

If Teddy thought you weren't listening to him, he'd holler at you.

"Turn 'em off!"

After that, I bet you turn them damn lights out.

Music was the backdrop to everything I did. In the morning, I woke up and brushed my teeth listening to K.C. and the Sunshine Band's "Boogie Man." That was like my morning cup of coffee. They couldn't help but make me happy—a group of guys calling themselves Sunshine. Come on, now! It doesn't get any better.

I went to my first concert when I was fifteen. I had to convince my mother to let me go with my cousin. It was a George Clinton-Parliament Funkadelic concert. Oh, man. I was so excited. And I learned so much that day. I found out that they smoke marijuana at those things. Shocking, I know.

As a matter of fact, at this particular concert a huge joint was lowered onto the stage. It was the size of the Goodyear blimp. It puffed and talked in a voice like the Wizard of Oz.

The giant joint said, "DO YOU WANT TO TOAST THE BOOGIE?"

That must have been a signal of some sort, because all of a sudden people pulled out joints and passed them around the audience. Everybody had one. I was completely unprepared for this moment. It wasn't like my mother sat me down and said, "Listen, when someone asks, 'Do you want to toast the boogie,' it means . . ."

She told my sister about cramps and backaches, but I didn't get a single word about a contact high. When I left the concert I was feeling good, you know, just from being in the atmosphere. I also came home with a souvenir—a joint, which I stuck in my sock. It felt safer there than in my pocket.

My mother was waiting for me when I came home.

"How was it, baby?" she asked.

I glanced at her, but I couldn't answer at that moment. I was overwhelmed by a strange urge to get undressed and eat cereal. I couldn't think about anything else. I went directly to my room, took off my clothes, and came back out into the kitchen wearing only underwear and socks.

My mother watched in silence while I got down a big bowl and filled it with cereal. I was oblivious to her. I couldn't wait to eat the bowl of cereal, maybe the even the whole box.

I thought I was being cool. Taking care of business. Not doing anything unusual. Just a man satisfying a powerful need. But mothers see everything.

"What is that?" she said.

Huh? I looked at her with bewilderment in my eyes. "Did you say something?"

"What is that in your sock?"

Man, I couldn't believe my bad luck. Before I took my first spoonful of cereal, I was in trouble.

I wanted to say, "Mom, I'm so hungry right now, don't make me explain."

But I knew I had to explain, and I told her everything.

Then I got the Toast the Boogie speech.

The next time I'd have an experience that amazing at a concert was around the time I was graduating from college. Sade was playing the Fox Theater in St. Louis, and I was more than a fan—I loved that woman. On the night of the show, I was sitting around my apartment wishing I had tickets. It didn't sit too well with me that my girl was in my town and I wasn't going to see her.

Irritated, I put on my best suit, tie, grabbed my car, and drove down to the theater. I waited outside, watching people as they went inside. There was one old lady taking tickets. Every time she took a ticket, she turned away from the door and threw it away. The next time I saw her do it, I quickly walked in right behind her back.

I went straight to the floor level. I told the usher my wife had already sat down. They believed me, let me pass, and I found a seat in the eleventh row. It was a sold-out concert, and nobody came for that seat the whole night.

Sade was magical. She came out barefoot and looking beautiful, singing like an angel. I was in awe. Mesmerized. Entranced. At one point, I swore we made eye contact. The way things worked out told me that I was supposed to be at that concert. But then something even more wonderful and unexpected happened.

Before the show ended, one of her people tapped me on the

shoulder and brought me backstage. I waited outside her dressing room while she changed clothes. She had me get in her limo and ride back to the hotel, where we made passionate love for two days, living only on champagne, chocolates, and each other. Naw, I'm just bullshitting you—but can't a brother dream, damn!

CHAPTER FIVE

GETTING SCHOOLED

My high school was mostly black, but we also had a large percentage of white students. It was around sixty-forty. A few years before, it was the other way round, but black families were moving from the inner city to the suburbs, so even though there were trees and lawns and homes with white picket fences, it was still the hood.

Despite obvious segregation in Caruthersville, the black and white folks got along. You didn't hear much talk about racism even though it was there. For some reason, people didn't take comments that would cause riots today as anything more than typical dumb-ass redneck shit.

For instance, you'd have a good old boy, the kind who had his name on his belt buckle, "Billy Joe Bob Earl," and an unfiltered Camel in his mouth, and he didn't know better than to let his mouth run.

"Hell, I like blacks. I got a pair of black boots. A black pickup truck. I even got a colored TV."

That's when you had to hit him in the face.

"Now you have a black eye, too."

The things that kind of guy did for fun were not amusing to us, and you could hear those Jim Bobs bragging about what they did on the weekend.

"We were outside the other day, and I'll tell ya, my brothers came over, Arliss and Jacob, and we got to drinking. We drank so much that we went over to the colored side of town and got to yelling racial epithets: 'Coon! Porch monkey! Go back to Africa!' You know, the standard shit.

"Well, you know they got up and beat the living crap out of us. One of them threw me through a plate-glass window. Severed the tendon in my shoulder. Look it, I don't have any movement in my fingers. But I'll tell ya what, that was the best goddamn time I ever had in my life!"

That describes your basic racist in the town where I grew up. The guy who hated you for being black was also the guy who was bragging about his limp. They were too dumb to get really mad at.

"I fell off the back of a calf and it drug me down a gravel road about five miles," Jim Bob would say. "I couldn't get loose. My boot was caught. Man, it skinned me so bad I had to take skin off my butt and put it on my back. But I'll tell ya what. You couldn't have had more fun than me on that day!"

I had a lot of fun in high school. I acted in plays and worked on the yearbook. Most guys played sports, but I was more social. Okay, I was kind of a nerd.

I was studious because my mother wasn't having it any other

way. You couldn't bring home a bad grade when your mother was a teacher. But even doing well in school, I still had no idea what I wanted to do with my life.

During my sophomore year, I got a wake-up call when all my friends began talking about college. I wasn't thinking beyond the spring musical. The next year they got really serious about their college preparations, which scared the crap out of me. Not wanting to be left behind, I jumped onto the college bandwagon and took the SATs.

What a frightening test.

Talk about going through a change of life. One day you're trying to figure out if James is ever going to get a job on *Good Times,* and then the next day you're taking a test that determines the rest of your life. At sixteen, you're not ready for all that.

I didn't pay attention to people who argued that the test was biased against blacks. I thought it was weak to be making excuses before you even got your scores back. I was like, "Dawg, ain't no big deal, just another test."

Then I saw the test and read the first question:

DIVISION: TRAVESTY
1. imitation: ersatz
2. release: trouble
3. proposal: gift
4. scan: procedure
5. daydream: rejection

I jumped straight up out of my chair. "Get me Jesse Jackson on the phone! How's a brother supposed to get into college answering this biased bullshit?"

Then I got to the math: "If a planet the size of Earth were a perfect sphere, and a television cable were made to circumscribe its equator, dividing the planet into two equal hemispheres, approximately how many feet of additional cable would be needed to elevate the cable exactly one foot above the surface of the planet?"

Television cable?! We didn't have cable TV in the hood. You couldn't buy that shit at the barbershop.

"Never mind Jesse, I need Johnnie Cochran!"

CHAPTER SIX

GIVE ME MY CREDIT

I wanted to go to an all-black college in the South, but my mother wasn't confident about me going that far away, and she turned out to be right. After my first semester at Southeast Missouri State University, my grade point average was—how does the number 1.2 sound?

It was at Southeast Missouri that I met my manager-to-be, Eric Rhone. After my sophomore year, he came to the school from Pine Lawn, a rough part of St. Louis. And he thought he could come to the school and just run things. Which was pretty funny, because the brother was small in stature, light-skinned with freckles. But what he lacked in size, he definitely made up for in attitude and heart.

He was really bold and different than what you would expect from a character his size. And we hit it off from day one. He grew up around gangsters and had a real tough demeanor. He was real crazy.

One time we were driving back to campus from St. Louis

and his car broke down—just died about three miles from campus. He was so mad that he went into the trunk, pulled out the crowbar, and proceeded to whoop that car's ass. He busted out the windows, beat in the fender and hood. He took off the license plates, and when one of our friends came to pick us up, he left the car right there on the highway. He never looked back.

They used to call Eric "Swan" or "Swannie" because he was so smooth, he sort of floated around campus. And we became so close that if you saw me without him, someone would ask, "Where's Swannie?" We were like the campus Abbott and Costello or Lewis and Martin. We were a comedy team for sure. We would sit in the cafeteria every day and snap on everybody coming in the door. He was real cool and fun.

There were a lot of cool people at my school. And the diversity of people I met was an education in itself. One of my roommates was Kelly Keene, from Kenneth, Missouri. He was a good old country boy. He was the nicest guy in the world. He got so cool from hanging out with the black kids, but it got weird when Kelly would come in a room and say, "What up, my nig-gers?"

Black people use the N-word differently than white folks. But he didn't understand.

"Yo, my nig-gers, what's going on?"

"Kelly, Kelly, Kelly, bro, we gonna have to get you something else to say."

"What's going on? Why can't I say it? I'm down," he'd say. "I'm one of the fellas."

"But when you say it, it's too, well, it's too twangy. Yours has too much *er* sound, and it should be more of an *ah* sound."

I was majoring in communication and taking courses that would help me in a career in front of the camera. I took a lot of television classes. I thought I was going to be a big news anchor.

In my senior year, I interviewed with a CBS affiliate. I'd gotten through a couple of interviews, so I saw myself going on to become the black Dan Rather. I didn't want to get caught doing weather somewhere, so I heard myself delivering the world report in a way that was slightly different, one that made sense to black folks.

"Well, folks, today the U.S. bombed Iraq. I mean like, babow! We blew that motherfucker up! In other news—but this is real deep, so y'all might want to sit down for this . . ."

Needless to say, I didn't get the job. And I needed it, too, considering some credit problems I was having at the time. Like a lot of college students, I got hooked up with credit before I was really able to handle it.

I never realized how important good credit was, even though my mother always preached that to us growing up.

"Even if you don't have a lot of money," she'd say. "If you have a good name, you can get anything."

People would say that my mother was rich because we always had things. And she would say, "No, I'm not rich, I just have a good name."

A good name started with good credit. Good credit means paying off all your credit cards, and when you owe somebody, you pay them on time. That's what messed me up. My bad credit came with two words: American Express.

When I got my first little credit cards in college, I was doing fine paying them off with my work-study jobs. I could pay them ten dollars one month or twenty dollars the next and handle that. So when I got my American Express, I was like, "Cool!" I couldn't wait to use it. That was the card that said you were a true playa. You whip that out and people know you got money.

The first time I used my American Express card was on a lady. That's a lethal combination—women and credit cards. And I got caught out there.

When I graduated, I came home and I wanted to go out on a few dates, floss, and act like I was living large. I started charging suits and dinner (something that I had never done before). I was acting all suave while I was out to dinner with this young lady—ordering up everything. "Yeah, yeah, go ahead and get that," I said. "I got you."

The bill comes, and I don't even look at it. I just threw my American Express card up there. Her face lit up, knowing she was with a real player. I gave her one of those looks that said, "Yeah, I'm a grown-ass man."

The bill was like sixty dollars. The suit I charged for the date was like two hundred dollars. The flowers were thirty dollars. I put some other random stuff on there, too. When I got the bill, it was five hundred and sixty dollars, and I couldn't pay it. I tried to pay it down. But the thing that I didn't know about the American Express card is that you have to pay it all off at the end of the month—all of it. They want their money. They don't play.

I barely had twenty dollars in my bank account. Let me say the scariest letters in the alphabet are "I-O-U."

If you don't pay American Express, you get that letter that says, "Listen dawg, come up with the dough—the entire amount, partner—or else we're gonna ruin your credit for life. You won't be taking ladies to dinner no more. You'll be serving them dinner."

I had lost a job selling fax machines shortly before that bill came. And I really, really couldn't pay the bill. Here I was with a college degree, no job, and an American Express bill I couldn't pay.

It took me a while to get another job. I was living off my other credit cards. I finally got a job selling electronics at Best Buy. But I was mad—I had gotten a college degree so I could sell Walkmans and cameras and stuff, waiting on Christmastime so that I could make some real money?

It took me two years to clean that up. And American Express wouldn't give me another credit card until last year: "Yes, you are a two-time NAACP Image Award winner, no you cannot borrow five hundred dollars!"

CHAPTER SEVEN

LIFE ASSURANCE

Now, before I became this big-time comedy star, I was just a regular workingman. After college, I had real jobs.

I was an undercover security guard at Sears, which was an ignorant-ass job when you think about it. How is somebody going to steal a refrigerator without you seeing them?

"Hey, partna, I see you with that washer and dryer! Where do you think you going?"

The job was easy, but the problem was that I had too many friends who thought they could just come in and take stuff because I was there. They would come into the store and give me the signal like, "I'm here, don't worry about it. I got this."

"Bro, I'm the security guard," I said. "You can't do that. This is my job."

"Ced, where's your loyalty? Are you with the hood or have you sold out to Sears?"

I lasted there six months.

Then I went to work for State Farm Insurance as a claims adjuster. After people had accidents, I was responsible for assessing the damage. I was the guy who stood between the wreck and the check. I decided whether we were going to total the car, repair the thing, or do nothing. I was good at the job. I became a specialist. They called me in to handle the special cases—irate black folks and owners of Corvettes and Mercedes.

The Corvette and Mercedes drivers were the worst people in the world to deal with. They thought their car was the most important thing ever created. They'd be like, "Man, I don't care that I hit that animal. My door's got a ding in it. I need a whole new door!"

"I ain't giving you a whole new door," I'd say.

"But this is a Corvette, man. I pay all this money for insurance. You aren't going to just paint over it!"

"Sir, calm down. Let me talk it over with you. You've got to come back in. If you walk out, I can't help you."

"Okay, all right."

"I'll tell you what we're going to do. We're going to fix it up. Do a new paint job on it. We're going to paint the whole door, not just the spot. We're going to make sure it looks good. If you don't like it, then we'll talk about a new door, okay?"

"You're going to paint the whole door?"

"I'm gonna paint the whole door, bro."

I had such a cool, mild-mannered style. And I was kind of comical. They would call me in before they'd get a supervisor. I was basically a problem solver. And this job was full of problems. Actually, it was nothing but people with problems that needed solving. People in car accidents lose all perspective. Not only is their car banged up, so is their brain.

Someone would come in with '72 Vega, a car that cost around eighteen hundred dollars to fix. The Blue Book value of that car was twelve hundred dollars. The car was totaled.

"I don't think it makes sense to fix it," I'd say.

"What do you mean? This car's a classic!"

"No, it's a Vega. This car is light-years from being a classic. A car's got to be at least twenty years old to be considered a classic, and I don't know if a Vega will ever be considered anything except old."

They gave me the irate black people because they spoke a totally different language, and I was the only one in the office well versed in it.

When black people get upset, we don't like to negotiate. We just want to yell and intimidate folks. We go straight from "What do you mean I don't get a whole new car" to "If you don't give me a new car, I'm gonna come back and blow up your whole motherfucking building!"

"Come on, man," I'd say. "No one's ever heard of a black guy blowing anything up. They won't let us get ahold of no C4. No black man can walk into a store and buy some explosives. So just settle down and let's talk."

I knew black folks were just making threats, but the fact is we say that kind of stuff with such conviction that it scares the shit out of people.

I was considered bilingual—I spoke regular English and angry Negro. I'd be called in to talk to the brothers and get them to cool off. I always started with the same tactic.

"Bro, I know you're angry, but do you want to get arrested? You'll never get your car fixed. Instead you'll be posting bail."

"But—"

"Calm down 'n let me talk to you. First thing, bro, you can't get your taillights repaired by threatening to kill everyone in the office. The people who run this office don't particularly like writing checks to people who cuss them out. They'd prefer to send your ass to jail."

"I don't want to go to jail."

"Okay, then let's lose the bomb threats and start over."

The most dangerous situations occurred when the company didn't want to pay a claim. I'd find myself acting like the Crocodile Hunter. I'd sneak up to a room and start narrating in an Australian accent: "What we have here is an irate black man. My supervisor has advised me that we're not paying his claim. We do not feel like we're at fault. This could be very dangerous!"

Then I'd go inside, holding my little notebook.

"There's more! This bad boy has brought his cousins! It's turned into a very tricky situation. Hey, guys, wait in the lobby and let me talk to my man."

I just happened to stumble onto this talent one day when the office was hit with a double whammy—a black Corvette owner. It was one of those days when all the supervisors were at a big luncheon, so no one was there except an assistant manager guy. I knew instantly he was in over his head when he ran upstairs babbling about how we were all going to die. He said something about explosives. The whole office tensed up.

"What's the matter?" I asked.

"I got a Corvette owner," he said, panicking.

"Yeah?"

"And he's black."

"Quit shaking," I said. "I'll handle it."

I went into the room with the guy and did what no one else in the office could do—I pulled the race card: black man to black man.

"Come on now, brother," I started. "Let me talk to you, man. I know what it's like. You don't really have no dynamite, so quit saying that."

I calmed him down. He left the building. I returned to the office a hero. Everyone thought I'd saved their lives. From then on, I was the go-to guy. I was the Harvey Keitel of claims. My boss, Mr. Winston, would hand me a file.

"What do we have here?" I'd say. "A black man with a Lexus. All right, I'll tell you what I'm going to need. I want two supervisors on each post, there and there. I'll need an ink pen and a check. What're we talking about paying? By the looks of the situation, I need clearance to go up to at least fifteen hundred dollars. I'll start at nine hundred dollars and I'll try to stay under twelve, but if I can't, I'll raise the price and we'll solve the problem. Are we agreed? Does everyone understand me? Good. I'm going in. . . ."

CHAPTER EIGHT

THERE'S NO BUSINESS LIKE . . .

I got into show business as a *Soul Train* dancer. I was with that little Chinese girl with the long hair. But then I got into it with Don Cornelius and smacked his glasses off, and that was pretty much it for my dance career.

Naw, I'm bullshitting. I never got into it with Don Cornelius.

I started doing comedy about the same time I got hired at State Farm. It was around this time that Eric approached me about managing my comedy career.

"Career?! Whatever, dude."

Eric always had these big ideas. So he became my manager. We weren't trying to do a contract back then. We operated under the philosophy, "Do what you say you're going to do, and we're cool." That was fifteen years ago, and we've been together ever since . . . just doing what we say we're going to do.

That's rare in this business. But Eric was true to his word. He would be making deals, booking dates for me while working at a chemical company in St. Louis. So while I was still at State Farm, I worked at different clubs at night and on weekends, gradually building a name.

The more I performed, the more I found myself in a predicament. If I wanted to make it as a comic, I knew I had to quit my job at State Farm. On the other hand, my job was hard to leave. The company had been in a discrimination suit, so I got moved along real fast. By my third year, I was making forty thousand dollars a year and buying a little car, a little house, a little bit of this and that. Once I got to fifty thousand dollars, which would be the next year, I wouldn't be able to quit. The job would be too good. That kind of money in St. Louis?! Shiiiit!

At the same time, I was telling myself not to get trapped. I knew I wasn't a great claims adjuster. I let the regular day-to-day stuff pile up. There were mountains of paperwork on my desk. I was the specialist—good at going in and solving the hard stuff. But I didn't want to be defusing bombs all my life. I was looking for a sign. I was even going to church and praying about it.

I was at the height of my dilemma when the manager of the Funny Bones, a chain of comedy clubs headquartered in St. Louis, took a liking to me and booked me in all twenty-two of their clubs. He signed me to work in each of the clubs twice a year as the emcee for something like three hundred dollars a week. It wasn't a lot, but it was steady, it was solid, and it was comedy. It was also the end of State Farm.

"Cool, I'll take it," I said.

CHAPTER NINE

ROAD TRIP

I had three weeks before my first date in Davenport, Iowa. I decided to make the pilgrimage to the land of la-la, Los Angeles. I had an '85 Ford EXP, which had tinted windows, nice rims, and a stereo system that made me think it was some kind of cool-ass sports car. It was really just an Escort. I got in the car by myself to drive like thirty-six hours to L.A. Well, I actually drove thirty-two hours to Las Vegas first, so I could visit my old college roommate. This road trip was the first of many times that comedy has afforded me to the opportunity to see the country. Since then, I've traveled to many a small town, many a backwoods, and it doesn't matter where you are in the country, you can always tell when you're in a black neighborhood.

When you're driving down the street and see a church, a liquor store, and a Chinese restaurant on the same block, you're in a black neighborhood. It's always the same. You show me any Dr. Martin Luther King Jr. Boulevard and I'll show you a church, a liquor store, and a Chinese restaurant. Sometimes, though, there's a slight variation—a check-cashing place is thrown in, too.

This fact got me thinking about how my neighborhood back home had a lot of Chinese restaurants. We would hear rumors about how they saved money by cooking stray dogs and cats. I never knew if it was true and didn't want to know, but you know what? I did see an awful lot of children walking up and down the street calling, "Fluffy? Fluffy? Here, boy! Hey mister, have you seen my dog Fluffy?"

"No, we see no Fluffy."

Then you go into the restaurant and see item No. 23 on the menu is "Fluffy Fried Rice."

I'll tell you something else people don't like to openly talk about, but if you travel around the country as much as I have, you know it's true. There are a lot of fried chicken places in the hood.

Usually they're next to each other. You'll see a Popeye's next to a KFC next to a Church's. Church's is known for serving the biggest, most humongous pieces. You've got to know there's something wrong with those chickens. There ain't no normal chickens the size of rottweilers. These chickens walk around with chains on, they got muscles like Bow-Legged Lou from Full Force. It's just something that concerns me.

And then typically there's some neighborhood kind of chicken place, a local spot. But they don't just do chicken, they do several other things, like Harold and Raymond's Chicken and Photo Developing.

You see this all the time in black business. It's like we don't trust our original idea, so we have to add to it to make sure it succeeds. If we open a dry cleaner, we can't just stop there. We have to open a dry cleaner/tax office/video rental business. You drop into a barbecue joint and find out you can also get a lube and oil and buy a wedding dress, too.

I was in one of those places once, and I asked if I could get my nails done while I waited for my ribs and oil change. The guy said, "No, but you can go next door to the manicure/bail bonds/dental school clinic."

So after spending five days in Las Vegas with my old college roommate, I finally arrived in L.A. Unfortunately, I couldn't do any sightseeing, because I was due back in Davenport soon for my first gig. I just went to a comedy club where I saw Damon Wayans and the late, great Robin Harris. I also saw Joe Torry, who I knew from St. Louis. In those days, he was hosting *Def Comedy Jam.* He was a rising star. In my eyes, he had made it. Joe came up to me between sets and said, "Man, I can get you onstage. Do you want to go onstage?"

This was the moment I'd dreamed of, the door through which I'd go on to fame and fortune, following in the footsteps of the great ones. It was wonderful, unbelievable, a dream come true. This is what I had quit my job to do.

"Want to go onstage?"

"Naw, man," I said. "That's all right. My throat hurts." Really I was shook—scared to death!

The next day, I hopped in my car and drove back to Davenport for my first gig.

I was a little nervous, so I would have a couple of drinks to loosen me up. I did two shows a night. And I didn't know I only got two free drinks a night. By the end of the week, I had drank so much, I ended up owing them thirty dollars. Needless to say, I stopped drinking before I performed.

You must understand when I first started, I only had about five minutes worth of jokes. So I had to figure something out. I planned to tell stories, dance, recite poetry, and do whatever I could to get laughs. I would entertain.

Sometimes my poetry would be the best part of the act. I had a poem entitled, "Where'd You Get that Smile," and I would recite it in a voice like Barry White's:

The night was young
As I searched for my fish in the sea
Not knowing what I was searching for
But someone who would make my heart shiver with glee
And there I saw her
The epitome of beauty, the essence of light
Her hair so long, her dress so white
I ran to her as though it were my one chance
And led her to the dance floor as we began to dance
I held her so close as I let out a sigh of relief
And then she looked up to me and smiled
I said, "Damn, baby, you ain't got no teeth."

I figured I would really stand out with that one because not many people were doing comedy *and* reciting poetry. And while I had everyone's attention, I also figured I could give out insurance quotes during the show.

The theatre manager kept referring to me as "this next comedian." He would say, "This next comedian coming to the stage . . ." But I was more than a comedian. So I spoke with him about it. I told him, "I'm not just a comedian, I'm a comic-poet-singer-dancer-insurance salesman."

"Son, you sound like a black-owned business," he said. "I'll just introduce you as Cedric the Entertainer."

So the next time he introduced me, I was "Cedric the Entertainer." And the name stuck.

On that first tour, when we worked those little clubs, they housed all the comics in a condo rather than giving them hotel rooms. I was one of five guys in a two-bedroom condo. As low man on the totem pole, I was told the rules: The headliner got the biggest room, the midlevel guys got the other bedroom and living room couch, and I was given a closet with a futon.

"And my man," one of the midlevel guys told me, "in the morning, you've got to get the bread and make the coffee."

Was that written in the comic rule book? If so, I missed that chapter.

"I ain't in college, dude!" I said. "I'm not pledging no fraternity. Y'all on your own!"

"You don't know how it works."

"Brother, please!" I said. "I used to handle bomb threats."

The tour was going pretty well until I got to Dallas, where the manager of the Funny Bones club told me they didn't need me anymore.

"But I have a contract!" I said.

"So?"

I could diffuse bombs, but I didn't know how to deal with that. I'd spent about one hundred and fifty dollars getting there, and I had another one hundred and fifty dollars in my pocket. I needed the three hundred dollars he was supposed to pay me. I had been counting on that money—counting it in my head the whole time I was driving there.

That's how black folks are with money—always counting it before we actually got it. Take income tax refunds, for example. Every black person I know can't wait for that tax check to come. It's like a once-a-year lottery and everybody's a winner.

Then the check comes and everyone gets to talking about all the shit they're going to do with the money. People have so many big plans for that check. You hear them say, "When I get my check, I'm going to go ahead and put a down payment on my car, get my mama something nice, buy a big screen TV, then I'm going to open up a business, and give a little back to the community."

"How much are you getting back, dawg?"

"Eighteen hundred dollars."

So that's what I was doing. I had one-fifty and I was going to make three hundred dollars, then another three hundred dollars at the next club . . . suddenly zeroes were flying by. It didn't matter that I didn't have any of that money in my hands. I was going to get it, I was supposed to get it, I might get it. So in my mind, I had it. Suddenly, I was thinking, "Yeah, I might put a down payment on this Lexus."

But in real life, I'm stuck in Dallas. I drove around—past the church, the liquor store, and the Chinese restaurant—and I stumbled upon another comedy club. This club, owned by Steve Harvey, was one of the first black comedy clubs in the country, and it was really popping. I hadn't met Steve, but we'd heard of each other through friends, and on the night I walked into the club, the headliner happened to be bombing.

I told Steve my story, and he let me go on up and do five minutes. I got a standing ovation, and Steve had me come back the rest of the weekend. He paid me two hundred dollars. He brought me back a month later, and this time he paid me one thousand dollars as the headliner. My man had style. He even picked me up at the airport in a limo. A stretch limo no less!

That was the first time I'd been treated special. I tried to play it cool, like I was used to that kind of treatment. But come on, you can't help but go a little crazy the first time you're in a limo. They had better glasses in that joint than I did in my house.

CHAPTER TEN

MOVING ON UP

You know how black folks like to show off. When we get a little money, we like to make sure everyone knows we hit it. It's part of being ghetto fabulous. That's a big thing in the hood. You find people who have a little studio, nothing bigger than a matchbox. Then you go in and see a big-screen television, so big you got to watch it from the hallway. That's ghetto fabulous.

They've got a brand-new Cadillac parked outside, but the refrigerator is empty. She don't know how she going to pay her phone bill, but her hair and nails got to be done. Ghetto fabulous.

I had a cousin who sang in the Impressions when it was Curtis Mayfield and the Impressions and they were big. They used to come over to our house in a limo. I just knew he was famous. Then Curtis Mayfield went solo, and the rest of the Impressions wanted to know, "Where'd the money go?!"

"I don't know, man. One minute we were hot, the next minute we were not."

That's when I decided I needed to be careful with my money, because that's the reality of this business.

Before I made it big, while I was still doing comedy shows and working at State Farm, I had a brush with ghetto fabulousness. But I exercised more restraint when it came to actually buying. I had my eye on a classic '68 Cadillac convertible for sale in St. Louis. It was a cool car and I wanted it badly. I pictured myself driving around the country in luxury. There was just one little hiccup in the equation. The car was four thousand six hundred dollars, which was way too steep. I was just climbing the ladder. But that didn't mean I couldn't get the car—at least temporarily.

One day my manager, Eric, and I went to the classic-car dealership that was selling it and asked if we could take it on a test drive. We'd dressed up to look like serious players, hoping to fake them out, and it worked. Assuring them that I was serious, I told them that I wanted to get it checked out by my mechanic, who I swore was the best mechanic in St. Louis and worked on all my cars, as I glanced over at my Renault Encore.

For some reason, they didn't send a salesman with us. As soon as we got a couple of blocks away, we put the top down and went cruisin'.

"My mechanic's out to lunch," I said, calling in from the road. "So we're going to need the car for a couple of hours. That's all right? Cool."

Our first stop was Levine Hat Shop on Washington Street. We bought big straw hats. Six hours later, we brought the car back to the dealer. It was dark out. The engine was hot. The gas tank was on "E," and we'd put about three hundred miles on it. We were straight flossing. We took pictures and everything.

"What'd you guys think?"

I shook my head to show my disappointment.

"It's nice, but my mechanic thinks it needs too much work," I said.

Then we walked over to my Encore. The damn thing wouldn't even start, and we had to wait for someone to come pick us up.

The summer of '95 was the first time I had some real money, after years on the road doing shows. And I couldn't resist buying a Rolex. I know it's a cliché, but I'm a watch man. Rolex is the watch you always hear about as a status symbol of someone who has made it. So that's why I needed to have it. But I didn't go all the way out. You can pay a hundred grand for a Rolex. The one I bought was like three-thousand-something. My mom noticed right away.

"How much did that cost you?" she asked.

"About four grand."

"Four grand? You could've got a better price at the barbershop."

Now I thought I was on my way to blowing up. I was emceeing BET's *Comic View,* which I thought was going to be a springboard to real fame and fortune. I had so much desire to make it that I felt like I would do almost anything to get there.

But with that kind of success, you have to be careful. You don't want to cross that line. That invisible, thin line. That very, very thin line between folks saying, "We want you to be successful and everybody's got your back," and people saying, "You done sold out!"

The sellout factor is real with black folks.

It's like when someone complains, "There ain't no brothers doing the news."

And you say, "We got Bryant Gumbel."

"Ah, he sold out!"

When Michael Jackson was doing his *Off the Wall* album, everyone said, "That brother's doing good." By the time he dropped *Bad,* the tide had turned: "Ah man, he's sold out!"

Whitney Houston became a sellout by the end of her first album. When she sang "Saving All My Love," she was the pride of the African-American community. We loved her. By the time she got to "I Want to Dance With Somebody" and her pop appeal kicked in, the brothers were like, "Man, she sold out!"

And then she married Bobby Brown, and she got a permanent ghetto pass.

But I was thinking, no matter how big I got, I couldn't help but appear to sell out. People change. Do you think Bryant Gumbel still goes to sleep wearing a wave cap? Do you think he still likes a lot of sugar in his Kool-Aid? When he drives his car, does he lean to the right?

I finally decided to move to Hollywood when I was offered the job to host BET's *Comic View.* Once I got there, I could see why brothers sold out. L.A.'s soooooo expensive that you got to sell something. Eric and I decided to drive out to Hollywood from St. Louis. We found a house through a friend of a guy who had a friend who had a brother who told somebody who I knew, "Hey, I got this big house in L.A., so tell Ced and them that they can stay there."

We were like, "Cool, what's the address?"

Eric and I made a bet that we could drive all the way across the country with the top down on my brand-new convertible

Mustang, which I had bought with my advance check. That car was dope, 5.0, triple black—black car, black top, black interior.

Aside from making it to L.A., we wanted to live the wild experience of driving across country in a convertible. It was mid-August, so the weather in St. Louis was nice enough that we thought it was possible. We made it through Oklahoma, too. It got hotter in Texas, but we turned on the air-conditioning and slapped on the sunblock (Note: I couldn't afford to get no darker). But a strange thing happened in New Mexico. The temperature dropped.

"It's surprising how cold it gets here," Eric said.

"Yeah, I thought this was the desert," I said, my teeth chattering.

Freezing our butts off, we stopped and put on jackets. We drove a few hundred miles like that, with the heat blasting, trying to stick it out. Like two guys lost at sea following a shipwreck, we were really suffering when all of a sudden Eric looked at me and said, "Do you think we made it far enough with the bet?"

"We're not in the Midwest no more are we?"

"No, we're in the West," he said.

"Then I'd say we made it."

We put the top up immediately.

When we got to Hollywood, we were so excited. That was the place to be. They talk about blacks in Hollywood as being second-class, but let me tell you the truth. When you first come to town, you don't even start out that high. No one tells you, but there are steps. You have to work your way up through the different minorities just to achieve black status.

I started out among the Middle Easterners. The landlord of our new house, which turned out to be an enormous Mediterranean monstrosity still under construction in different parts, was a wealthy Iranian named Sammy. He popped in at all hours of the day and night to tell us nonsense. Then he'd flash a smile and say, "Me go now. Good-bye."

He sounded like the lady on the *Weakest Link* and always looked too happy.

"Why is he so happy?" we wondered.

Then we found out through the friend of the friend who had a brother who had a friend who helped us get the house in the first place that the rent was twenty-two hundred dollars. Sammy was getting rich off us! I'd just come from St. Louis where you never heard of that kind of money for rent.

"Are you serious?! That's how much it really is?" I asked Sammy.

He smiled. "It is true," he said in his thick, Iranian accent. "Me go now. Good-bye!"

Soon, the guy who got us into the place eased out of the arrangement, taking a trip to Dallas that was supposed to last only the weekend. But the dude never returned. Neither did his share of the rent. Suddenly, Eric and I had to shell out money we didn't really have, including all the utilities. Sammy began coming by hourly asking for money. Finally, I had no choice but to tell him the truth.

"Sammy, we go now. Good-bye!"

Upset, Sammy ordered us to move out. "I want you gone from my stuff," he said.

We hurried and loaded up my car with everything we had brought, bought, and shipped and tied it all down with string and rope. We had boxes, clothes, and lamps piled inside and threw the mattress on the roof. We drove down the street looking like a couple of Mexicans.

We found a little townhouse in a small complex in a gated community. Sammy was a memory. No Middle Easterners to be seen. Our new neighborhood was entirely Latino. We were moving on up.

A food truck would show up around nine or ten at night and blast its horn, which sounded like Woody Woodpecker's laugh. Sometimes the truck would come by even later. And when I heard that horn, I would say, "Why do these people need to buy fruit in the middle of the night?"

I figured out it must be code. You ask for a bunch of bananas, wink-wink, and a new TV was delivered. You order a couple of kiwis, and the next day someone parks a pickup in front of your apartment. It was the Latinos' version of buying stuff at the barbershop. It had to be, really, because who you know buying tomatoes at two in the morning?

The kids in the neighborhood looked like they were gang-oriented, but their parents wouldn't let them actually join a gang. They were really nice guys just acting tough. And I loved their nicknames. There was Sleepy and his brother, Little Sleepy. Puppet. And Chili. They were all right. And they took an interest in my career, too.

"Hey, is that Mustang your car?" they asked.

"Yeah."

"Okay, we'll watch out for it."

By hosting *Comic View*, I was able to make a living and create some star appeal, though it was limited to people who watched BET, mostly blacks and Latinos. I still wasn't known in the

Hollywood inner circle. I didn't have white executives wanting to see me, and whenever they did, I could tell they really didn't know who I was, even though they'd try to pretend.

"Hey, I've seen you. *Def Comedy Jam,* right? You're Charles the Interrogator. Funny stuff!"

There's another side of Hollywood that many people trying to make it end up seeing. I got my first glimpse of this on La Brea and Sunset when I saw all the cheesy motels with prostitutes in front and pimps on the pay phone in front of Denny's.

You'd glance into the manager's office and see a bunch of eight-by-ten photographs on the walls, all of them autographed by people you never heard of.

It made me wonder if Denzel and those kinds of guys had ever actually stayed in places like that, and then people used that to promote their businesses. In Hollywood, they'll promote anything associated with a celebrity.

The marquee in front of a ratty hotel will say, "$17.50 Per Night. Cable TV, Queen Sized Beds. And Samuel Jackson Slept Here Once."

Or you check out an apartment. A little studio.

"How much is the rent here?"

"This apartment doesn't look like much, but it has a star history," the landlord will say. "You know the guy who played the judge on *The Jeffersons?* And the lady who played Mrs. Roper from *Three's Company?* Well, they both lived right here for a week. It's a lucky place. That's why rent's six hundred-fifty dollars a month."

Shortly after I did my first movie, *Ride,* I had finally arrived as a black man in Hollywood. Finally, second-class status! I knew because I was hassled by the police. It happened after I pulled a U-turn in the middle of the street outside a nightclub, trying to impress a few ladies. Maybe it was more like a 360. Or several of them. But there was no need to call out the cavalry.

Suddenly, I was surrounded by five black-and-whites. I was scared to death. I glanced in the rearview mirror and saw Rodney King looking back at me. You can't ever be ready for a beating. But I braced myself for the worst.

Fortunately, when I let the window down, I saw the officer who approached my car was black. *Thank you, Lord!*

"Where do I know you from?" he asked.

"I'm Cedric. I'm the host of BET's *Comic View.*"

"Oh yeah. You're funny," he said. "I like you. I think you're going to be big . . . but give me your license and registration anyway."

Damn!

CHAPTER ELEVEN

DEARLY BELOVED

I guess I have always considered myself a playa. I've always been a favorite with the ladies. I was sexy even before it was popular for a dude like me to be sexy. I came up in the era when the girls were going for the bowlegged, light-skinned, pretty-hair dudes.

I was none of those things, so I had a strategy. I had a plan. I made friends with all of the pretty girls. I would just be around them all the time, and I was real cool with them. I dressed nicely, I had a fun personality, and I had a car. The ladies had no problem hanging out with me.

I was what I call "long-walking" them. I was willing to take the long road for a beautiful woman, to climb mountains, to jump off cliffs. I'd be their friend, their cousin, whatever, just so I could be around them and brag to the brothers, "Well, yeah, her and me, we hang out."

And when one of those bowlegged, light-skinned, pretty-hair dudes messed up, I was the shoulder to cry on. And by the time Wesley Snipes and Michael Jordan started to bring back the darkness—made it popular to have dark skin—it was over. Even when I started to put on a little weight, that worked in my favor, too. I was cuddly and cute.

I never had a problem getting a date. I had what you call playa-energy, and it got worse when I started making a little bit of money and getting some fame.

I met my wife at the height of my playa years. As Ludacris and Nate Dogg's song goes, "I had hoes in different area codes." I had so many women it was crazy. I even had the nerve to have one girlfriend who allowed me to be a playa. She was cool with my philosophy. She didn't stress the fact that I was with other women as long as I was treating her right.

When I met my wife on the set of the movie *Ride,* she saw me coming. It was my first movie. I played a bus driver, and she was a costume designer doing the wardrobe. We shot most of it in Jacksonville, Florida, but we didn't actually meet until we came back to L.A. to finish up. She was cute—she still is very cute—and she had a real centered kind of energy. In other words, she had her shit together.

I tried to impress her by playing the part of a big movie star, but she wasn't fooled. She had worked on many films and had seen the stars as well as the secondary players like me come and go. When I asked for her phone number, she said no. Bruised, I left on a road trip that repaired my injured ego. *Hoes . . . hooooooooo-es . . . in different area codes.*

Several months later, I was back in L.A., chilling at a popular jazz club. I noticed this sexy lady at the bar. She was so fine I started taking off my socks before I even introduced myself. I was ready. For me, it was attraction at first sight. And there was something about her. I felt like I knew her.

I made my move even though for some reason I was nervous as hell. On the outside I had my smooth Billy Dee Williams thing working, but on the inside I was shaking like Don Knotts at a craps table. I ran through possible opening lines, though let's face it, by the time ninety-nine percent of us guys finally get the courage to say something, all that comes out is, "Wassup?!"

I managed two whole words: "Hey, baby."

She smiled, but it wasn't because she was feeling me.

"You know what?" she said. "That's exactly why I didn't give you my phone number in the first place. You have no idea who I am, do you?"

I didn't. But I played it cool.

"You do look familiar. Tell me your name and I'll tell you if I know you."

She laughed—kind of. Then she reminded me of how we worked together on the movie *Ride* . . . and how I'd liked her. And how I'd asked for her phone number. And why she said no.

"You're just a celebrity who goes after women, one of those women-collectin' machines," she said. "And I'm not going to be one of your little girls!"

Why is it that boys always like the girls who snatch off their Band-Aid? That quick pain is something we start to need.

I stood my ground, apologized, and then charmed her the rest of the night, eventually persuading her to give me her phone number. And when I called, she answered (luckily) and things went from there. It was a whole new experience for me. Not that I had not been out with nice girls before, because I had. But Lorna was different.

She was raised with her mommy and her daddy, raised right. She was a goody-two-shoes who visited her grandmama often, went to church, taught little kids in the summertime. She is one of those people where you say, "Are you for real?!"

So them little games I was used to playing didn't work. She was not having it. I was charming and we went out on dates, but the conversations were different. They were real. I mean, I was telling her things about myself I wasn't sharing with anybody. And we would get deep. We would have intriguing, intelligent conversations. She had her points and I had mine. That led us to being good friends.

The first time I realized that she may be "the one" came during basketball season. I usually went to the Lakers game when I had time with my boys. We would go basically to enjoy the ball and do some ballin' of our own, if you know what I mean. There were plenty of beautiful women at a Lakers game, and that became the spot.

One time, one of my boys couldn't make it for the next game. I had an extra ticket and I said, "I'm going to bring Lorna." Before I could get the words out of my mouth real good my boys looked at me like I was crazy. And I couldn't believe that I had said it myself. I would never, ever bring my girl to a game. That's where I would meet more ladies. But I wanted to bring Lorna. I meant it. It was genuine. I really wanted to bring her to the game. I would rather be with her than anybody else. And that scared me. We were getting serious.

I tried to back off. I told her, "I'm going to go on back. I still need to play a little bit." And we broke up. I went to try to be the playa-playa, going on some dates. I even flew a couple of chicks out to California to hang out, and the whole time I'm thinking, "This ain't getting it. I'm just miserable. I ain't feeling none of this."

They were all pretty. But none of them were bringing it home, they weren't doing it for me.

I called Lorna on the phone and we hooked back up again. And this time I knew she truly wasn't having it. I had to come correct. And after a couple of years, I had to make that move. The first thing I did was go over and speak to her parents. Her daddy is a college basketball coach, a pretty straightforward character. He used to be Muslim, so there couldn't be a whole lot of bullshit. He's a cool cat, though. I asked him and her mother for Lorna's hand in marriage. And they said yes.

Then I planned a trip, just a little getaway. I wanted to surprise her. I picked Lyon, France, because it began with an L. I wanted to go someplace that started with the same letter as her first name. (Yeah, I know it's corny.) I didn't want to do Paris . . . everybody does Paris.

We flew to Paris and then drove to Lyon, and she had no idea what was coming. I was so cool. She didn't know the setup. We had a driver take us through the countryside. We ended up driving to the Riviera. It was so romantic.

When we got to Lyon, I had it all planned. We would have dinner, and I would have the waiter bring the ring under the covered dish. It would be done with lots of formality and pageantry, like a Fred Astaire movie. The waiter would lift off the silver top, say "Voilà!," and in the center of her plate, Lorna would see a beautiful, sparkling, expensive diamond ring. She'd look at me lovingly, crying tears of joy, and the whole restaurant would applaud.

Well . . . that's not exactly how that scene went down. Lyon, unlike Paris, is really, really French. I mean folks don't speak a bit of English. And I don't speak a bit of French. I tried to give the waiter my instructions, but he had no idea what I was talking about.

So I had to improvise. I got on my knee, old-school style, and I sang a song to her that I wrote. Instead of the *voilà!* and all that, I ended up saying, "Hey, baby, will you marry me?" I knew she couldn't say no because I had her passport, and if she did, I was going to leave her in Lyon. She said yes and started crying (as planned), so it worked out fine. She loved the whole thing, but there was no *voilà!* I wanted the *voilà!*

We had a nice, big, lavish wedding at a grand old mansion we leased in Pasadena, California. The party took place under enormous tents. We had three bands, everything was decorated with flowers, and we blew it out with the best food. So many of our friends and family came—more for the mansion, the music, and the free food than the wedding—that scalpers were getting one hundred-fifty dollars for the good seats.

You know your family's either happy or just can't believe it when you start hearing uncles and cousins saying, "I'll pay good money to see this wedding."

My family coming in from St. Louis thought they were on the most amazing trip. The house, the bands, the food, the ambience of wealth. I had to watch them closely the whole night. I had aunts who actually missed the ceremony because they were wandering around the house. During the vows, I could hear them saying, "Ooooh, look at that stuff. What do you think they paid for that?!"

All night I had to run behind them.

"Get out of that woman's cabinets! Put those forks back up!"

Thankfully, it wasn't your typical ghetto wedding. If you've ever seen that, you know what I'm talking about—a true ghetto wedding, between two ghetto-ass people who love one another. That's a scary sight. Groomsmen are coming down the aisle in silk short sets with matching wave caps, or matching formal do-rags with studs. All the bridesmaids got on lime green dresses that break away into bodysuits, like they were sixth men coming off the bench.

Then the flower girl comes down aisle, but she ain't got no

flowers. Her basket's full of sunflower seeds, and people are picking them up and eating them as fast as she throws them down.

Cut to the groom: He comes down the aisle all cool and normal, his head bobbing, just kind of smiling, gesturing, and muttering, "Hey, dawg, it's cool, yeah, it's cool."

Then he turns and waits for his beautiful bride to make her entrance. The bride is walking down the aisle with a pair of mules that are two sizes too small, so her heels are just hanging off the back, and she's trying to keep them on even as she's tearing up the crepe paper they put down. This is her show. She's Whitney, Janet, and Beyonce all in one for the entire day. She's got on a gown that's a little too short and has too many colors going on. She's also got every hairstyle known to man happening at once—dookie braids and crimp curls, sister curls, a flip wrap, and one them little T-Boz bangs over one eye.

She starts out coming down the aisle to the traditional wedding march, but then the deejay mixes in Luther Campbell's 2 Live Crew bass beats—blasting from the hidden speakers—and sets the party off.

"Get on and shake your booty. Come on and shake your booty."

All of a sudden the bridesmaids trade looks. They're like, "Oh, shit, we're about to make a little change up in here!" And they start dancing like they're at a strip club.

Later, at the reception, the newlyweds get their gifts in grocery bags. They have a German chocolate cake with a little bride and groom on top doing "Tha Butt." Shortly before midnight, the cops come and the groom has to sneak out because he's got warrants.

Marriage is tough nowadays. Couples just can't make it, can't stick it out. One of my favorite couples right now is Bobby and

Whitney. You can say what you want about them, but they're still together. No matter what we think about them, they're still surviving. And there's something to be said for that.

To me, that's the measure for getting up and doing anything in life. If your ass is tired and you don't feel like going to work, just say to yourself, "If Bobby and Whitney can stay together, I can get my ass up and go on to work."

If you and your lady are having problems and can't seem to work them out, just think, "If Bobby and Whitney can stay together, we can make this thing work."

CHAPTER TWELVE

BABY, BABY, BABY

One of the happiest times of my life was when my wife had our son.

I was excited. It was big responsibility. There was so much to worry about—and that was before the baby was born!

There are all of these myths people have about pregnancy and babies—like figuring out the sex of the baby. If she's carrying low and craves Gummy Bears, it's a boy. If she starts to snore like a grizzly bear, it's a girl. And if she starts loving show tunes . . . well, you know what to expect then.

I took all this stuff seriously. My wife would say I was a little bit too serious. When she went into labor, the pains were coming every minute or so, and I was a nervous wreck.

"Cedric, baby, relax a little bit."

I said, "Okay, sweetie, breathe."

She acted like she was ignoring me, so I was more emphatic.

"Breathe!!!"

I took Lamaze classes, and they said she had to breathe when she went into labor. So when we got into the real deal, I tried following the book to the letter when really—and they don't tell you this—you have to let the woman lead. But I had this under control.

At a certain crucial point during labor, my wife said, "Baby, look at me!"

"Are you breathing?" I asked.

"Relax! Just hold my hand!"

I realized that she was really holding my hand to help *me*. She was keeping *me* calm. She was helping *me* get under control.

"Everything okay now?" she asked.

"Yeah, it's better."

"Would you be quiet now?"

"I'll try."

Then she turned to the nurse and said, "C'mon y'all let's do this. Let's have this baby!"

My wife was in labor for about twenty-five hours. I have no idea how my wife felt about it, but I'll tell you this much, it was a long time for me. I sat there, trying to roll with her screams, her pains, her pushes, and feeling so helpless. Finally, the doctor came in to check and asked how things were going.

"I think I'll make it," I said.

"Excuse me, but I'm talking to your wife."

She was screaming at that moment, so I answered for her.

"She's doing okay."

I have never known my wife to take artificial painkillers, not even an aspirin for a headache. She's a real health nut. Vegetarian. Eats organic foods. But she turned to the doctor and said, "Y'all better give me something for this pain!"

Then the baby starts to come, and the nurse says, "Can you see the baby?"

You act like you're looking, but you ain't really looking.

"Yeah, yeah, I see him," I said.

Could I see the baby? Hell no, I was dizzy, trying to keep from passing out. Then the doctor asked if I wanted to cut the umbilical cord. That caused me to snap.

"Hey, did the whistle blow?! Is it quittin' time?! Why are you leaving work early? Hell, no, I do not want to cut the damn cord."

But I cut it anyway and even watched the circumcision. *Ouch! Sorry little dude, but you'll appreciate this when you're older.*

PART II

THE WISDOM OF A GROWN-ASS MAN

CHAPTER THIRTEEN

THE PAPER CHASE

When you have money, you become your own color. Money transcends race. Everybody hates the rich. And what's funny is that no matter how rich you are, it's never enough. No matter how much money you have, there's going to be someone with more money. You think Michael Jordan's rich, but then there's Bill Gates's money that just puts Michael's money to shame.

I have a nice home and a nice car, and when I travel I fly first-class. But there are folks that have their own private jets and fly when they feel like it, while I'm standing in line at United Airlines. That doesn't sound like much to complain about, but when you have to fly as much as I do, there are some things that start to bother you.

When you board a plane, you give up all your rights. They never tell you the plane's mechanical history or if the pilot's had a fight with his girlfriend or if he had too much to drink the night before or not enough sleep. They don't tell you that you'll probably be sitting next to someone who hasn't showered in a week.

They just want you to jam your butt into your seat and wait.

They tell you to turn off your cell phone, your two-way, your computer, and your Gameboy. They say you got to shut off all electronics during takeoff because that's the most dangerous part of the flight. But if you ask me, the most dangerous part of a flight is the first twenty minutes it takes for people to be seated.

Let's face it, everybody rushes to get on the plane and nobody's happy with their seat. People get on the plane and all they want to do is change seats. You can feel the tension. First you got the switchers—the people who are flying with their relatives or friends and couldn't get seats together. They walk up the aisle while all the other passengers are still walking down the aisle trying to find their seats. They're like salmon swimming upstream, looking for sympathetic people who'll switch.

Then you have the seat fillers. They got stuck next to the bathroom or in the middle seat between two heavy people and spend the whole time before takeoff watching out for empty seats. You can spot them by the way their heads turn side to side, like radar. The second the door shuts, they're up and running around the cabin, screaming, "Mine!"

But the worst part of flying on a crowded plane is having to share an armrest. A grown-ass man doesn't give up his armrest. I'm just throwing that out there. It's the most precious turf on the plane.

People get in fights over this shit. It's as bad as road rage. People ain't got nothing else to do for three hours except push each other's arms. We've all been in that situation. You don't talk or look at the other person. You don't even acknowledge their presence except by increasing the pressure. It's ugly. But a grown-ass man is not intimidated.

You have to find some control where you can on a plane, because the flight attendants have all the power. They give that talk about what to do in an emergency and expect people to pay attention. One time I was on a plane, and the flight attendant was giving her little speech, and I never looked up. She got to the part about what to do if the cabin loses pressure and your oxygen mask drops, and she saw my reading light was on.

She stopped talking, walked over to my seat, turned the light off without even asking, and gave me a look that said, "And? What you going to about it?!"

But I refused to be intimidated. I said to myself, "I'm a grown-ass man, and you can't just turn off a brother's reading light! You lucky I got this seat belt on!" I had to say that stuff to myself, because they *will* take your ass off the plane in handcuffs, no doubt.

That's why I need to make more money. I got to keep chasing that paper so I can get enough to buy me my own jet.

Money's a problem at every level. It's never enough. Even the folks on the street corners holding up the signs saying, "Hungry. Will work for food," want more. I say to them, "Playa, we all working for food!"

You give them a dollar, and they say, "Ain't you got any more?!" I'm kind of amused by them. I might actually give them more money if they were more honest. How about holding up a sign saying, "This is my job!"

The worst are the crackheads. I'm not talking about all crackheads, because there are many who are living quite well in corporate America and the entertainment business. But I'm talking about the crackheads who live in crackville.

I would give one of them money—just to keep him out of my neighborhood. But if you give a crackhead money, you won't ever get rid of him. He'll keep coming back. And if a crackhead stays in your neighborhood long enough, you'll eventually get robbed. There ain't nothing worse than when a crackhead robs your house.

You can always tell when a crackhead breaks into your house because they steal dumb shit like the CD cases—just the cases—

one tennis shoe, a can of beer, and all your black socks and belts. That's crackhead stuff. They steal stuff you don't really need until you need it. Then it makes you mad when it's gone. At first you're happy that they didn't steal the TV. Then you're getting ready to go out to a club and can't find a belt. "Damn, crackhead!"

Crackheads steal dumb shit and then try to sell it for one dollar.

"Yo, partna, where's the CD?"

"It ain't there, man," he'll say. "That's why it's just a dollar. Please, bro. I'm a crackhead. I don't want to have to break into your house and steal one of your slippers."

If you know a crackhead, they think they're real good at covering their shit, but they always give themselves away. Like they're coming by knocking on your door at four in the morning talking about, "Man, I need $2.56 to go to Milwaukee."

"You going to Milwaukee right now?!" And you know it's $69 round trip on Greyhound. Where is this fool going to get another $66.44?

"Are you riding a bike to Milwaukee?! Man, are you on drugs?" That's where they break—in the cross-examination.

"No man, I'm serious!" he'll say. "I wouldn't come by here if I wasn't serious."

"Brother, you on crack! Get out of here!"

But even a crackhead is just trying to get more. I understand that mentality of wanting more. I'm as guilty as anyone when it comes to that. I'm trying to get my money on like everyone else—by playing the lottery.

People hear that and say, "Ced, you already got money." But

I don't have two hundred million dollars, though. That's how big the lottery gets sometimes. In some states, I've seen it even higher. That's real money. That's buy-a-jet-and-not-have-to-stand-in-line-at-United-no-more money.

You can always tell when the lottery starts getting up there. At around twenty million dollars, white folks have their housekeepers buy their tickets. Over seventy million dollars, white folks actually come to the hood in person. You see them at the liquor store, looking nervous, waiting on their numbers.

I don't blame them. Like I said, no matter how much you have, everybody wants more. Anytime the lottery gets to be more than twenty-five million dollars, you're subject to see me at the store scratching quick picks.

Now, if I won, I'd keep it real. That's how you know I'm a true Cadillac-type playa. If I got all that cash, I'd do the right thing. I wouldn't be ignorant. I'd put most of it in the bank, invest in stocks, bonds, certificates, and what have you. But I'd carry about thirty-six thousand dollars in cash on me—true playa style. And it would be in a rubber band, too, dawg.

I'd keep that knot in my pocket while I went around doing everyday things. I'd go get my haircut.

"How much is that? Ten dollars? Right on, dawg."

Then I'd pull out the thirty-six grand, slowly undo the rubber band, and search for a ten. Same thing at the gas station. The knot would come out and I'd peel off a few small bills.

"Uh, let me get a pack of Newports, two more lottery tickets, and give me three, no, go ahead and make it *four* dollars on pump eight."

The lottery aside, we're part of a new generation of African Americans who are starting to understand wealth. Our grandparents may have been poor. Our parents were workers who maybe went to college but worked their asses off to send their kids to school. And now we're part of a generation that's actually making money. There's not just a black middle class, there's a black upper class.

I remember the first time I met with a financial planner. My family was proud of that. They were more proud than when I got my college degree.

"Ooou, you know what that means? Ced's loaded!"

That was hardly the case. I'd simply been talked into meeting with a financial planner whose first question to me was, "How are you planning for the future?"

"Huh?" I asked. "What do you mean, planning for the future?"

The financial planner went on about different plans, wills, and what have you.

You know black folks. We want to spend all of our money now. White folks like to discuss "the future." For blacks folks it's "Tomorrow ain't promised to no one, I'm going to spend my money now!"

White people hope they live long enough to spend all the money they put away—money they can't touch until they're sixty-five—while black folks wish they had money to spend right now.

"I'm going to be candid with you," I said to the financial planner. "I don't plan on leaving people a lot of damn money."

That caused him to explain how people keep wealth growing in their families. How people keep the wind blowing. He asked me to suppose my grandmother left me one hundred thousand dollars. Then he explained that if I left thirty percent of that to my children, they'd be rich by the time they were my age. They'd be swimming in so much money, they'd start talking with an English accent.

"But that can't happen," I said.

"Sure it can," he said. "At sixteen percent, compounded annually . . ."

I could see smoke coming out of his calculator.

"Excuse me," I interrupted. "If my grandmama left me a whole hundred grand, my kids are going to have to understand that I'm going to spend it. I need to enjoy that money."

Eventually, I worked out a plan I felt was right and fair. I figured out a way to take care of my immediate family. As for everyone else, I arranged to leave them what I called "just enough." If they've got cable TV, I'm leaving them just enough to keep it on. If they don't have cable, they ain't getting it. If they got a car, I'm leaving them just enough to get them back and forth to work. If they don't already have a car . . . they won't be able to get one. That's the only money I'm leaving behind.

Otherwise, my financial plan calls for me to take it all with me. The government is going to be upset when I die. There ain't going to be nothing left. At my funeral, my relatives will be checking under the casket. When no one's looking, they'll be shaking my dead body, whispering, "You know Ced be having that fat knot. Check his pockets!"

But there won't be a dime left. I'll be in my hospital bed saying, "Forget life support. Hook me up to eBay!"

My last words will be, "Bid on that big screen for me."

But you know who doesn't need a financial planner? Oprah. Oprah Winfrey is probably the richest woman in the world.

GROWN-ASS MAN

They say she's got like a billion dollars. If she's like most black women, that ain't the half of it—she's got some more stashed away somewhere . . . just in case. Check her underwear drawer. Maybe some shoe boxes.

If you watch her show, you know that every day she talks about all the shit that makes you happy—your spirit, your relationship, your self-image, your weight.

Hey, I'm a grown-ass man. Not being broke makes me happy!

CHAPTER FOURTEEN

CAN WE ALL GET ALONG?

I don't really understand racism and hatred. I don't hate anyone. In fact, I've spent a lot of time trying to figure out how we really are the same, and after lots of thought I think I've come up with the one common denominator, the one thing that will bring us all together: ribs.

White people love ribs. Black people really love ribs. The Chinese love them, too, as long as they can dip them into hot mustard. Maybe the key to getting along is having a big barbecue.

Now, the Latino community has got some weird shit going on between them. I had a housekeeper, and I made a mistake and said she was Mexican. She got all indignant and said, "I'm from San Salvador." Then I hired a nanny from Mexico and didn't realize that there would be trouble. I'd wake up in the morning, and there would be some shit going on in the house. I felt like a NATO peacekeeper just trying to get my coffee. I didn't get it. Both of them were nice women. They both spoke Spanish. They should have gotten along. Then they show up one morning armed to the teeth. I had to get a metal detector by the front door. I felt like I was at a high school, not my home. It was crazy.

Then there's Cuba. I watched with interest as America lost its collective mind over little Elian Gonzalez. Even I was tripping off that little Latin boy. I felt sorry for him. But he needed to go home.

I'll tell you what the trouble was, though. They were trying to send the boy back to his daddy in Cuba. Look, I grew up in a divorced family, and the truth is, nobody wants to live with their daddy! Your daddy's stuff just ain't right.

He ain't never got two clean towels. Barely any soap either—just a sliver. He's got peanut butter but no jelly. He's got a washer but no dryer.

On top of all that, Elian's daddy was living in Cuba. Everybody's trying to get their ass *out* of Cuba. They're trying to escape by any means they can think of. Boats, rafts, plywood, cardboard box. They don't care. They just throw a piece of dry-wall on the water and go. They get an old inner tube, put five families in it, and start paddling, screaming, "A-me-ri-ca!" *I want to be in A-me-ri-ca . . . life is so free in A-me-ri-ca . . .*

Yeah, I felt bad for Elian. But let me say this, if that little Latin boy had been from Haiti, it would've been a whole other story. He would've been thrown back in the water faster than you can say, "We don't need any more black boys, so you go right back to your daddy."

There's one group that no one's talking about anymore: the Indians or Native Americans. It's probably because there are very few of them left. They got shafted about four hundred years ago when the Pilgrims came over supposedly in peace, and it ain't been right for them since.

They showed the Pilgrims how to farm, how to eat, how to

stay warm, and what do they get in return: smallpox, murdered, and put on reservations after their land was stolen.

Thanksgiving? More like the Indians asking, "After all we did for you, this is the thanks we get?!"

After all they been through, Native Americans are finally getting their due—the three or four who are left. They figured it out. Today if you are an Indian, you get free land and you don't have to pay income tax. I don't know which Indian figured it out, but whoever it was ought to be in the history books alongside Sitting Bull and Crazy Horse.

No income tax! Shiiiiit! That's why so many blacks be trying to claim they got Indian in their family. And you don't see that commercial with the Indian crying anymore. They have their casinos, their no-tax cigarettes. They are living large.

CHAPTER FIFTEEN

HOPING AND WISHING

The big racial rivalry is still between blacks and whites. It's like the Yankees and the Dodgers. We're two different organizations with long histories and different philosophies. Like white people can charge concert tickets. We've got to wait until the first or the fifteenth when we get our checks. And we're not putting tickets on no credit card. That's for big shit—like the outfit to go to the concert.

White people, they sit up front, right in the first rows. They order their tickets early; they don't wait until the last minute. And they make sure they are in those front row seats early. They come way before the show even starts because they know us. They know we'll sit in their damn seats. Then they got to get us out, and that makes them very nervous because they don't know how to talk to us.

See, white people live by a different creed than we do. White people hope things don't go wrong. They've got high hopes. Lots of hope. If they run a little late for a show, they think, "Oh my

God, we're running a little late. I *hope* no one's in our seats. I don't want any problems."

When you see the usher coming down the aisle with the flashlight, it's usually white people they're helping find a seat. White people get the usher because they don't want no trouble. They come in with the usher off the top. Because they hope things don't go wrong.

Black people rarely get the usher. We don't need the usher because we don't live by the "hope" creed. Black people are a little more confrontational about things. We don't do a lot of hoping. Black folks wish. We *wish* someone would be in our damn seat.

A brother comes to a show late and he's like, "I wish a motherfucker would be in my damn seat! As much money as I had to pay for these tickets? I *wish* a motherfucker would be in my shit."

Sure enough, people have their behinds in his seat.

"Hey, hey, hey, that's us, partna. Yeah. Seats four 'n five. Come on now."

And the brother wishes that person would say something stupid and not get up.

For white folks, it's totally different. When they're driving and realize that they've made a wrong turn and end up in the hood, they immediately start hoping. They hope things don't go wrong. They hope they don't get carjacked. They hope they don't get shot. Even when nothing happens to them, they're still hoping.

A brother rides through the same hood with a completely different attitude. He's saying to himself, "I *wish* a motherfucker would try and take my shit. I just washed my car, too!"

It's simply the difference between whites and blacks.

It's why gas and electricity never gets cut right off in the hood. We know we're late paying the bill. But when the gas man pulls on our street, what do we do? We walk out there on the front porch and say, "I know this motherfucker ain't gonna try to turn my shit off! I *wish* he would!"

White people are down at the gas company, telling a sob story, hoping they don't get shut off. We're in the street, threatening the worker.

"I'm cooking corn bread right now, dawg. I *wish* this motherfucker would try and turn my shit off."

You know another difference between blacks and whites? You hear about large groups of white folks getting killed. The last one I heard about had something like nine of them going down. All shot together.

But you never hear any news about ten black people getting killed all together, and you know why? It's because we run. We run when somebody else runs. And we don't be asking questions while we're running. We don't know why we're even running. We don't need to know. We don't need a run coordinator to get all the running organized.

If I'm with you and you start running, then I just start running, too. That's just how it goes. I'll wait till later to find out why we're running.

I ain't lying. Black folks can be in a group, dawg. Not even paying attention. Having a conversation. Got their dress shoes on. Holding a bag of groceries. Just going on about their life. Then a brother runs past. Dude just runs by for no apparent reason. And everyone takes off.

Woosh!!

Be like the start of the one-hundred-meter dash at the Olympics. Maybe longer, depending on how long people run. When somebody stops, everybody else has to stop too.

"Damn, dawg, you scarin' me," you say. "What the hell was we runnin' for?"

"Because that dude was running."

"They almost get us?"

"Don't know. I just took off."

Meanwhile, white people walk straight to the trouble: "What the heck is going on?"

One person follows the other until it's too late.

"Hey, what's the—" Bam! Smack! Blam!

Then like seven or eight of them get shot, and one of them is always like, "Why didn't anybody tell me?"

It's up to us to tell them, "Damn, dawg, didn't you see us running . . ."

Black people are still waiting on their payday. There are a lot of people talking about reparations for slavery. When black folks were freed, we were supposed to get forty acres and a mule. Hell, I would be happy with forty acres in Beverly Hills and a few blocks on Rodeo Drive. Give me the square footage and I'd call it even. No grudges.

I know a lot of black people have ideas about what they want in reparations. I got a call one night from some poll taker talking about a proposed referendum on reparations. He's lucky he got through. Most times when phone solicitors call the house, I either hang up on them or give the phone to my little boy. They're always calling when I'm settling in to watch TV. But on this night, I spoke to the dude.

"What do you think about the government making reparations to African Americans for the crime of slavery?" he asked.

"Hmmmmmmmmmmmm," I said.

"We're trying to get a measure on the ballot. Brother, do I have your support?"

He was serious. From his tone, I guessed he was the militant type. And you know how much black folks love to get behind a cause. We'll march over just about anything—an unjustified shooting, affirmative action, the closure of a Church's Fried Chicken, freeing Darryl Strawberry.

"Just because you're doing well, brother, doesn't mean you ignore the holocaust of history," he said. "You have to under-stand, we must save the children. We have to save our genera-tion. We're supposed to get what we're owed . . ."

Okay, I could get with that. My great-great-grandmother was a slave in Tennessee. Her husband was a slave. He was also part Indian. Suddenly, I envisioned myself owning casinos.

"How much are we talking in reparations, partna?" I asked.

"We're talking about pride," he said. "We're talking about justice. We're talking about four million slaves in the South, and millions more who died on slave boats. We're talking about repa-rations to right one of the great crimes in human rights history."

"Hey, playa, I understand, but can you tag it with a dollar amount?" I said. "I'm about to miss *106 and Park* on BET."

"You can't put a price on slavery," he said. "There's no price that can right the wrong!"

"Listen, bro, I need to hear a dollar amount."

He paused, and I sensed the weight of what he was about to tell me, the importance, the historical significance: "Twelve-hundred dollars on your tax return," he said. "Everybody would be rich. Think about the economic power we'd wield if every African American gets twelve-hundred dollars back from the government!"

I was speechless.

"Brother, do I have your support?" he asked.

I gave the phone to my little boy.

CHAPTER SIXTEEN

THE MALCOLM X GAMES

I'm a sports fanatic. I love watching sports, especially the Olympics. The 2000 Olympics from Australia was crazy, and I watched the whole thing, even the events that came on at three and four in the morning.

I was just surprised to see a black man pole-vaulting. That's not something you see everyday. It's usually an event for white folks. Because if more brothers learn how to pole-vault, you know we're going to be using it for evil.

Come on now! You tell a brother he can actually jump up two stories, he will figure out a way to use that to his advantage. Our baby mama never could get away from us.

We'll be outside yelling, "Kiesha, Kiesha, I know you up there. All right! Don't think I can't get up there!"

Then we vault up three floors to her bedroom balcony, taking stalking to new heights.

I tuned into the X Games once. I thought it was some kind of tribute to Malcolm X, but it turned out to be a bunch of white people skateboarding and bike riding—some real wild stuff. And I like those X Games.

But if you grew up in the hood, you had games far more dangerous than anything they were doing. I call them the "Project Games." We'd do gymnastics tricks on old mattresses that were piled up in a vacant parking lot. Not only would the springs be sticking up, the parking lot was full of glass, bricks, and nails. You'd have to do whatever trick the guy in front of you did.

"Yo, I'm gonna do a triple somersault on this pissy mattress."

It was like you'd better not miss your mark or else you'd be subject to all types of shit—tetanus, salmonella, ptomaine poisoning, and gangrene. There was no telling what would happen if you did a back flip.

We had bike tricks, too. We would see how many people we could fit on the handlebars and still ride downhill without someone falling off.

There were other events, like the Accuracy Throw. That was where you took a rock and threw it at the moving metro bus. And the Pit Bull Sprint. That was when the scary-ass pit bull that was usually behind the chain-link fence escaped and chased all the kids down the street. You had to run until the damn thing was either shot or ate one of your friends.

Now those were real extreme games. I want to see those dudes from the X Games survive that!

Golf used to be a white people's game, like pole-vaulting and skateboarding. That was before Tiger Woods. Now black people are stretching out. We aren't just playing basketball anymore. We're all over the place. Ever since Tiger took over golfing, we're out there trying to play, too. At least I am.

I see a whole bunch of black people at the golf course

nowadays. I call it the post-Tiger Renaissance. Seriously, we are hitting the links strong, boy. We're making white people nervous because we'll be at the golf course changing the game. We even show up looking wrong.

We're out there with wave caps on and shit. Brothers are wearing Timberlands and are out there barbecuing on the seventh hole, trying to borrow people's golf cart to run to the store.

"C'mon, playa, I'll be back. It ain't like it's your cart. Damn, let me just run to the store."

You know what this post-Tiger Renaissance means? More things are going to open up for black people in golf. First you're going to have more black players, and then we're going to have black golf announcers. That'll really change things.

A black golf announcer—I mean a real brother—would be a little more excitable about stuff. That's why we don't really do golf—because, you know, you've got to be too quiet. People are out on the course shushing you, and that's not going to go over big with a black announcer.

"Shushing me? I'm a grown-ass man, dawg. I can say what I want. Tiger's my cousin. I'm Darnell Woods. I can say something. Don't be shushing me, partna!"

A black golf announcer would certainly bring some spice to the game. This is how it would be: He may start off following the rules, talking real quiet and proper like the traditional announcer.

(In a hushed voice) "Tiger Woods, now on the eighteenth hole, is about to win it all. The crowd is tense. If he hits this putt, it'll take him to nine under par and the victory. This very short putt should break a little to the left. He steps up to the ball and . . . and . . . and—"

(Yelling) "DAMN, DAWG! YOU ALMOST HAD THAT SHIT! TIGER MISSED THE DAMN PUTT! I'M SORRY, PLAYA. I DON'T KNOW WHAT TO TELL YOU."

It's not just golf that we're taking over. Venus Williams won Wimbledon. Serena Williams won the U.S. Open. Soon we're going to be doing all their little sports. Next thing you know, we're going to be downhill skiing. And won't need any skis, either. You know us. We'll be out there in church shoes. Brothers will be on the slopes in a pair of burgundy Stacey Adams.

We're taking over sports, dawg. Next thing you know, we'll be doing equestrian, synchronized swimming, water polo. Even hockey. Actually, I don't know about hockey. A couple of brothers are already playing that sport. But I don't know if they are going to let some real brothers play hockey. You know, like Bolo, Nuck-Nuck, Crazy D, and them. In hockey they let you fight, so you know, if we start getting in the game there's going to be a brother out there skating without a stick. Just angry and wanting to fight. He'll be walking around, not even skating, saying, "I *wish* a motherfucker would try and hit me with a stick."

Once we get good at those fancy sports, then we might just have to start an all-black country club. Oh my goodness! If you have an all-black country club going, it would probably start out right. But eventually, it would just turn into a nightclub. The parking lot would be full of low riders and Benz's with twenty-inch rims.

And you could never get into the club. People would be coming in and out with a stamp on their hands. There would be long lines out front, with brothers saying, "I know I'm not a member. But my name's supposed to be on the list. Check the list!"

The pool would be empty. And golf would be secondary.

Instead, people would be playing football on the grass between the eighth and ninth holes. There would be pit bulls, rottweilers, a big old German shepherd named King guarding the cabanas.

Eventually, the outdoor part of the club would turn into a park. That's just how we do it.

CHAPTER SEVENTEEN

BLACK ENTERTAINMENT

Have you ever been to the movies when there are a bunch of black people in the theater? That's the craziest experience. Black folks don't care what they're going there to see. We go to the movies to talk. We get to our seats, sit back, eat the popcorn, and just start looking around—waiting to comment on something.

If we know the movie is going to be like three hours long, we'll bring our own food. It'll be a full buffet at the front of the theater.

Someone'll be asking, real loud, "Who made this potato salad?! I don't eat just anybody's potato salad."

The second the lights go out, we start talking. We shout at the screen, telling the actors what to do, and we holler at each other. We're all a bunch of shouters.

You can't enjoy a movie because you got someone in there talking on a Nextel two-way with his homie.

Beep-beep.

"Yeah, what up?"

"Where you at?"

"Watching *Matrix 2*."

"Yeah? Me too. Where you?"

"About four rows back. Wassup?!"

"Wassup!"

"Dawg."

"Dawg."

"Know what I'm sayin'?"

"I know."

"All right, beep me 'fore you go."

That's why I don't like going to the movies with my people. When I go to the movies, I have to drive out to the suburbs if I actually want to hear what's going on in the movie.

I barely heard a word the whole time I watched *How Stella Got Her Groove Back*. The trouble is, you can't shush a black person. They're not going for it. I mean it. You just can't tell a black woman to stop talking when she's having a conversation with Angela Bassett. I wish someone would try it and see if they live to tell about it.

Here's what I figured out, though. When black folks talk in a movie, it's because we got common sense and we hate it when a movie plays like the audience ain't got no damn sense. That's why at crucial scenes you'll hear someone say, "Oh I hate this part—she's getting ready to go in this room and get killed. It's so stupid."

"Damn, please, can't you keep it to yourself?"

"Is that you, dawg?"

"Yeah."

"Get me on my two-way."

This ain't a big deal, but I can't let it pass. Why is it that movies with predominantly African-American themes are never made into ice shows for our kids? You'll see the *Lion King*, for sure. And there's "*Beauty and the Beast* on Ice." But you'll never see "*Booty Call* on Ice." Or "*Boyz 'N the Hood* on Ice." Or "*The Kings of Comedy* on Ice." (I don't know . . . that last one might have worked.)

But we shouldn't discount the idea. Imagine something like "*Set It Off* on Ice," a show about some female bank robbers going crazy, and it's an ice show. I bet that would work. That's something I see people getting into.

You know what's been strange to me for a long time? How much white people like space movies. It's kind of weird, almost obsessive. Black people don't really do space.

White people love movies about the moon and Mars and shit, and it's because they want to leave our black asses here on Earth. That's what they think. It ain't gonna happen.

Y'all move to the moon, dammit, we going to the moon, too! Oh, we be right behind y'all in space shuttles with Cadillac grills, chrome wings, rolling through space. One headlight'll be out. Tags will be all wrong. The whole solar system will be shaking from the bass in that bad boy.

Y'all know we can drive a space shuttle, too. That shit's right up our alley. A space shuttle is long. We grew up driving long cars. We would drive a space shuttle like it was a '72 deuce and a quarter. Get us a cigarette. Window down. We'll be leaning back, one arm resting on the window with Snoop Doggy Dogg blasting through the galaxy. We'll pull up next to the space station and gun the engine.

"Wassup?!"

White astronauts will be thinking the same shit's happening to space that happened to their golf courses. They'll get on the radio back to NASA so damn fast.

"Houston, we have a problem."

"Yeah, we want to stop in, have a malt with y'all. We'll be headin' to the moon to hit a few golf balls."

But the king of entertainment is still TV. It's rough in television for black folks. Even if you have a job, most brothers don't expect you to keep it. A guy came up to me and said, "You're on *The Steve Harvey Show!*" That was cool. "I saw you, saw the Image Awards!" That was tight. I felt good. But then he said, "When you gonna blow up?" I was like, "Damn, dawg."

It's not like I'm planning on blowing up. I can't afford to. There aren't a whole lot of opportunities for black people on TV. We haven't got it like white folks. They can quit their shows and feel confident they'll land on another series. They leave *Ally McBeal* and *ER* and go on to become movie stars. But you don't see us on one show and then see us pop up on something else. Only Uncle Phil from *Fresh Prince* gets to be on everybody's show.

Where's Webster? Where's Link from the *Mod Squad*? Where's Coco from *Fame*?

I'm a grown-ass man, and I know if I leave it's over. Next thing you know, I'll be hanging out with Rog and Rerun from *What's Happenin'*. If I'm on a show and it's cancelled, I ain't going nowhere. It's going to be like when your girlfriend tells you to pack your shit. I'm just going to sit there and say, "Look, I paid that cable. I ain't going nowhere until the end of the month."

When I was growing up in the late 1960s, early 1970s, I never noticed the color of anyone on television. And it didn't matter, either. I just wanted to watch. Like most kids, when it came to television, I was like an alcoholic. You know an alcoholic don't care what they drink.

"No gin, what about vodka? Only peppermint schnapps? Fine, give me some."

I enjoyed everything on television. But I had my favorites. *Happy Days.* I was a big fan. I loved the Fonz with his motorcycle and leather jacket. Plus he had that cool girlfriend Pinky Tuscadero. Even Richie was cool in a corny kind of way. I liked his family situation, too. They had the whole deal, mom, dad, Richie and Joanie. Now Joanie, that was my girl. I had a thing for Joanie. I'll just put that out there and see what, if anything, happens.

I also liked watching *The Dukes of Hazzard.* They had that cool car and rode around doing jumps and shit. *Starsky and Hutch.* Those cats were cool, too. So was the *Six Million Dollar Man.* I never once thought about the brother's color. All I cared about was that my little GI Joes could do the same thing that Lee Majors was doing.

I watched *Good Times* and enjoyed it as much as *Three's Company.* Good comedy is color-blind.

I'll tell you when television changed for me, when I first started tripping off the whole racism thing—that was in 1977. That was the year ABC aired *Roots.* Alex Haley's *Roots* changed television for black folks forever.

My parents had grown up with racism and the civil rights movement, but I was a post-1960s kid, which means I grew up with a watered-down picture of black life as something between

Good Times and *The Jeffersons*. We knew there had to be more to it, from listening to Marvin Gaye, but *Roots* was the first time we saw the whole picture.

I was in the ninth grade when *Roots* aired. After two weeks of watching Kunta Kinte getting his ass whipped on, I was more aware of color on television. Or lack thereof. Suddenly, I started asking, "Why doesn't Joanie know any sisters?"

"Why doesn't Mister Roper rent to any black people?"

"Why can't the Jeffersons keep a son?" They must have had five or six Lionels before the show was cancelled.

Even now, television needs more diversity. It's still segregated. Specific networks have black shows, but the major networks are still pretty white. Take the hit *Who Wants To Be a Millionaire.* That's a cool little show, but they hardly ever have any black folks on. Like we don't want to be millionaires?! Hell, they could give away thousands, and a brother would be happy. They could call it *Who Wants to Be a Thousandaire* and we'd show up.

Come on now. If I won sixteen thousand dollars, I'm out of there. I ain't going to press my luck.

"I just need enough to get my car out of the shop, dawg, and give my baby's mama a little change, and I'm cool."

And you can win sixteen thousand dollars on *Millionaire* with no problem. The first couple of questions are always pretty easy, like: "Old McDonald had a what?"

But even with questions that simple, people still have trouble coming up with the correct answer.

The answers would be: A. yacht. B. supermarket. C. hat. D. farm.

Contestant: "Old McDonald—hmmm. He couldn't have

had a yacht. There's no way he had that. A supermarket. Now, that is out of the question, too. A hat? Maybe. Hmmm. But I'm going with . . . farm. Regis, I think Old McDonald had a *farm*."

I get entertained just listening to people think out loud, and I get upset at how stupid they are. I'm at home yelling at the TV, "Damn, dude! Ignorant ass! You don't need to take all that time for that!"

I know why they don't have black people on that show. I understand. If they had black folks on *Millionaire,* it would be a whole different show.

We would have used up all of our lifelines by the second question. And forget about calling a friend. If we call somebody up and they don't know the answer, we're going to be like, "Hook Lisa up on the three-way and ask her."

"Sorry," Regis will say. "But it's one call. You can only make one phone call."

"What? What are you talking about? I can get my whole damn family on with one call."

I'll tell you another reason they aren't in a hurry to put black people on *Who Wants To Be a Millionaire.* We'd be forgetting everyone's phone number. When it comes time for the lifeline, we'd give Regis the wrong phone number. And you know how black people get on the phone. Even if we call the wrong person, we won't let on that it's wrong. We're on national TV.

Ring-ring.
Him: Hey, hello.
Me: Hey, wassup, dawg?
Him: Hey, wassup?
Me: What's up, man? Who this?

Him:	This is me. What's up, homeboy?
Me:	Oh, I thought this was you, man. Wassup, man?
Him:	You got it.
Me:	You didn't sound like you at first, man.
Him:	Yeah no, you know me man, I'm just chillin'.
Me:	You know who you talking to?
Him:	Yeah!
Me:	Who?
Him:	You, man!
Me:	Oh okay, it's me man.
Him:	So what you been doing?
Me:	Man, just chilling man, you know me, just hanging.
Him:	So you seen Steve?
Me:	Steve?
Him:	Yeah.
Me:	You talking, little Steve Johnson?
Him:	No, no, Burger Faced Steve.
Me:	Oh yeah, Little Bump Face Steve. I saw him the other day. He was with Tammy.
Him:	He was with Tammy?
Me:	Yeah.
Him:	Tammy Johnson?
Me:	No, you know, Big Booty Tammy.
Him:	Oh yeah, the one who be with Kim.
Me:	Kim?
Him:	Be with Kim, right?
Me:	Kim? Oh, Funky Breath Kim! Oh right.
Him:	Yeah, back up cousin.
Me:	Yeah, it's all good. Your brother Mike there?
Him:	My brother?
Me:	Yeah, Mike.

Him:	Man, I ain't got no brother.
Me:	Ah man, I thought this was you, man.
Him:	Nah not me, man. Call another time.
Me:	Later y'all.
Regis:	And so your final answer?
Me:	I ain't got one yet. Your people backstage dialed the wrong number!

And even if we do get the right number, there's a good chance that our lifeline will have their phone service shut off. Then you got to page them and hope they call back in time. "Regis! What's the number up here, man? I'm gonna page somebody. Give me your code, Regis." You know it would go down like that, too.

One reason we can't be on a lot of those shows is because of the language barrier. Nobody but us knows what we're saying. Remember the controversy about Ebonics? I understood the uproar. I knew why white people were up in arms. If black folks had their own language, we'd start whooping white people at things like Scrabble and *Wheel of Fortune.* That would be it. You'd start seeing Pat Sajak on the WB.

But think about this. We got words no white folks can pronounce, let alone spell.

For instance: Libela. As in, "I'm *libela* bust yo head if you don't give me my damn points." And lemme. As in, "*Lemme* use another lifeline, dawg." And what about naw? As in, "*Naw,* I ain't the weakest link, punk!" And 'n. As in, " '*N* now since you voted me off, I'm libela beat yo ass!"

Another show that won't have a whole bunch of black folks on it is *Survivor.* I got hooked on that show—those crazy people living in the outback, eating bugs and rats. That wouldn't work with a brother. We just gave up pork, how are we going to eat a damn rat?!

I'd be like, "I had to give up bacon for a rat? Come on, dawg! Ya'll don't even need to drop me off. I ain't going."

You want to know what survival is for me? Trying to live without color TV, TiVo, and NBA Live on Sony Playstation.

Then there's *Temptation Island*. What's up with that? I tried to get into watching it, but I couldn't. Maybe because the show's about America selling itself outright, and that's sad. Consider the premise: Get some happy couples together and see if we can break them up with some really sexy ladies and handsome dudes, while the rest of us watch their lives go to shit. Well, on second thought, maybe I missed something good.

There was one black couple on that show, right? And what happened to them? They get disqualified. For what? They supposedly lied about having a child. If you ask me, they probably didn't lie. Maybe it went down like this:

"Do you have any children?"

"Why you want to know?"

"It's a question we ask all potential couples."

"Why?"

"Because if you do, you can't go. That's the rules."

"That shit's discriminatory. How'd you like to see the Rev. Al Sharpton and about one thousand angry black folks converging on your damn island?"

"Okay, you're in."

Of course, my favorite form of entertainment is music. A true player knows the old school, but it seems like today is all about hip hop. That concerns me. You can't slow dance any more.

What happened? It's like everybody's waiting on the fast song—*shake ya ass, show me whatcha workin' with . . .*

When I ask when we're going to get around to old-school romance, I get told, "Don't nobody slow dance no more, dawg. It's all just thumpin' and bumpin'."

Some of these dances today are so sexually explicit they should charge $9.99 just to watch. When I watch BET's *Rap City,* I feel like I should get out my credit card. By the end of the month, I would probably have racked up about three hundred dollars in charges.

Let's face it, nothing stimulates the imagination like watching them dance on *Rap City.* But I'm a grown-ass man. I like to slow dance. It's old school. It takes a lot to get a slow dance. You can't thug up on no slow dance. You can't walk up to a lady and say, "Get yo ass out here and let's go!"

You've got to be nice to a person to get a slow dance. You don't see that so much anymore. I used to love getting a slow dance. At the club, I'd be waiting on the right cut to come on. Sitting with my partners, I'd say, "Yeah, playa, see Red Dress over there? Soon as my song comes on, that's me right there. I'm telling you, son, as soon as my cut comes on, I'm gonna be all up on her."

When that song came on, I'd put on my best will-you-slow-dance-with-me smile.

"How you doin? Okay baby, I got what you want, I got what you need. You wanna get this slow dance? Uh, you don't slow dance? Your friends got you holding their purses? That's all right, that's cool. Nah . . . maybe, you know, I'll come back and get you on a fast record or something. Next time, you know. Don't worry 'bout it."

I'd turn around. *She's trippin'!*

A second later I'd see her friend, "How you doin, baby? You wanna slow dance? Yeah, come on, hey, dance with me, baby. You lookin' good, yeah . . ."

Then you finally get that dance, and you spend most of the song trying to see how far you can slide your hand down to her booty.

But rap music is cool, too. It's evolved. Everybody's in on it now, but it started out in New York with dudes like Cool Herc, Grandmaster Flash, and Kurtis Blow. Kurtis Blow was the man: "Damn sucka! Sucka, rah! Rah! Rah!" How come nobody does that "Rah!" any more? That's a real loss.

New York rap is a trip. They got their own slang and everything:

"Yo wazup, son? Thas what I'm sayin, knaimean? Thas what I'm sayin! That's what I'm sayin, B, that's what I'm sayin, yo. Know wha I'm sayin? Thas wha I mean. Thas what I'm sayin. Knaimean? Word. Yo, God. Yo, Son. Know wha I'm sayin?"

No, I don't know what you're saying, dawg! It sounds like you keep saying, "That's what I'm saying. You know what I'm saying?" But I don't know what you saying when you say that's what you mean.

Southern rap's interesting. People like Cash Money, Master P, Mystikal. I'm amazed they could have records come out that have people saying nothing more than "Uhnnnnn, nanana. Let me hear ya say, 'Uhnnnnn, nananana!' " They got a whole song right there and blew up with that. All I can say is, I wish I had thought of it. Because I can make a whole lot of little sounds.

It's like they pulled some guy off a dirt road, some guy named Jethro or one of this cousins and said, just make some noises:

"Don't worry about what you're saying. Just get in the booth and make a noise."

"But I don't know what to say!"

"You like girls? Talk about them girls."

"I like them girls, mmmmmm, mmmmmm . . ."

"Great, we'll make something out of it."

I first started liking rap music when I moved out West. That was when Snoop Dogg started rapping. Snoop was my man. He sounded so good, so blazed. He sounds like he's smoked just enough chronic, making him rap so damn slow that even grown-ass people could understand what the hell he was talking about.

Snoop blew it up. He had everybody digging rap. He even had old Jewish white men digging rap. You could tell. They'd be riding in their car singing, "Rolling down the street, smoking endo, sipping on gin and juice, Shalom, dawg!"

Then we got groups like Bone Thugs-N-Harmony. They rap too damn fast for me, man. They rap so fast that when they first came out, I thought they were Spanish. Even though they're from Ohio, I didn't know what the hell was going on. I thought they were a new Taco Bell commercial. "Heynoburritocom-tito'nsourcream." I was like, "Drop the chalupa, dawg!"

Sometimes I think that rappers try to live out their lyrics. I'm tired of so many rappers getting in trouble, going to jail. What is it with rappers and jail, man? Are the acoustics that much better in a cell?

When I think about rappers and jail, I'm reminded of Suge Knight, CEO of Death Row Records. I don't know if he's really as bad as they say, but he's just become like a new millennium

Candy Man. I bet you can't go home tonight and say Suge Knight three times in the mirror.

That's a bad man right there. Even when Suge was in jail, I wasn't quite comfortable talking about him. Now that Suge's out, everybody's trying to get into jail. For months, people have been saying, "When Suge comes out, we're going in."

It'll be interesting to see how many guys come out of jail with record contracts. In fact, I was thinking, one day this hardcore rap is going to get old. It's going to play itself out, and a lot of these guys will end up getting married, having kids, going broke, and as so many people do at times of career crisis, finding Jesus.

I can imagine going to Snoop Dogg's church, where he's preaching, the Nuttin' But A G Thang All Good 4 Tha Eastidaz Missionary Baptist Church. "Tadizzle's scriptizzle is from Revelashizzle."

I really like reggae music. Reggae songs have a cause. They have meaning and power. There are issues going on in reggae songs. Real-life issues. If something's happening in those people's lives, they sing about it. Politics, revolution, religion, hunger . . .

> Woke up this mornin'
> 'N I was hungry, mon.
> Looked in the cupboard
> It was bare
> Oh no. Oh no.
> Oh no, mon.
> Thought I'd fix myself a sandwich,
> Had peanut butter but no jam.
> No jam, no jam,
> Oh no, mon.
> Help me now.

Peanut butter, no jam
Me hungry now
Peanut butter, no jam
Breakdown, breakdown . . .

I often think I could've been a songwriter. I could see myself writing semifamous blues songs about women I've loved. I can't play music, not even the harmonica, but still the titles come to me all the time. Like "How Can I Miss You If You Don't Go Away?" or "I'm So Miserable Without You, It's Almost Like You Were Here" and "Your Love is Like a Chicken Wing Without Hot Sauce, Tasty But Not Quite What I Want."

Remember Rick James? He was the man. The master songwriter. They said he wrote more than four hundred songs while he was in jail. None of them have come out, but I imagine they were all somehow related to his experience behind bars rather than his experience hanging out in bars. I'm sure they all had the Rick James "Fire and Desire" style. Maybe one of them went like this:

Put something on my books, baby
I need some . . . commissary

Another song, "Conjugal Visits":

Conjugal visits, conjugal visits . . .
Can't wait till Saturday
Conjugal visits, can't wait, mmmmm
No more two-inch glass
I'm about to touch that ass,
Conjugal visits, yeah . . .

Here's the start of another one:

> Twenty-two, twenty-three, twenty-four hours a day
> Your love's . . . got me on lockdown, baby
> Got me on lockdown, girl . . .

I grew up a big Michael Jackson fan. I was really into the Michael Jackson and the Jackson Five. Loved the Afros. Loved the cartoon. The dance moves were way before their time.

But that was when he had his first nose and original skin color. Nowadays his appearance has started to scare my kids.

A few years ago Joseph Jackson, the father of the whole clan, was sick. For a time, if I remember correctly, they thought he was going to pass. I imagined Joseph on his deathbed, calling the entire family together for one last Jackson family reunion.

"Gather around everyone. Tito. Jermaine. Marlon. Who's this one?"

"It's Randy, Daddy."

"Okay. Hi, Randy. Get Janet. Hey, Janet, you looking hot, baby. Where's Michael? Michael? Who's the white girl?"

"It's me, Dad. It's Michael."

"Michael? You look different. And is that eyeliner you've got on?"

"Yes, Pop."

"Michael, why you crying?"

"For the children, Pop. I'm crying for the children all over the world."

"Good for you, Michael. LaToya, put your clothes back on, okay?"

"Yes, Daddy."

"All you know you're my kids, but before I pass, I want to tell you something before you read it in the tabloids. We've got other family members. Though I never told you, I had a few other kids outside of y'all. Y'all hear of Jesse? Jesse Jackson? That's your brother. Can't sing or nothing, but he's a good speaker. He'll open up the concert. And then there's Rebbie Jackson. Did I mention Rebbie?"

"Yeah, Dad, we know about her."

"What about Action Jackson?"

Say what you want about Michael, but he started trends. The glove and the sparkly socks. The high-water pants. I know quite a few brothers were rocking those back in the day.

I know people want to give credit to Jennifer Lopez for starting the whole trend of wearing revealing clothes on national television, and God bless her. But she wasn't the originator. No, if we're going to be honest, Prince was the first one to do the whole J-Lo thing.

He was the first person to ever go on a national TV show, in this case the MTV Video Music Awards, and reveal some major skin. He had his whole ass out. Do you remember the ass-out pants? They were yellow—not that I looked too hard.

You've got to be Prince to walk around with those pants on. You can't be a regular everyday Moe at the gas station going, "Give me a lottery ticket and four dollars on pump eight."

Because when you turn around, the guy behind the counter's

going to say, "Sorry partna, but you can't shop here, not with your ass hanging out like that."

You can't wear pants like that to the PTA meeting. It ain't going to work. You can't talk about your kid having a reading problem and then walk out with your butt fully exposed.

The thing you have to realize is that the pants didn't come like that. Prince had to have those pants tailored. So at some point he was up on a box inside a three-way mirror, looking at himself and thinking, "I like these pants." But then he turned to his tailor and said, "You know Irving, the sequins are great. I love the way the bellbottoms flare out. And not putting any pockets in front, that's all groovy. But the pants need something else. I don't know what they need, but . . . hmmmmm. You know what, cut the ass out. That'll be perfect."

You can't wear something like that more than once. Does Prince then decide if he's going to give those pants to Goodwill or a family member? I can picture his nephew saying, "Uncle Prince, got anything in the closet you're not wearing anymore?"

Then Prince is rummaging through the closet and saying, "I've got these pumps. And those boots, I wore them in *Purple Rain*. You don't need those? Okay. Oh, you know what? I got these ass-out pants, and I only wore them once."

"Uh, no thanks, Uncle Prince. I don't think I can get away with those."

"You sure? I don't know where I can go with these ass-out pants. I wonder how I can get Jennifer Lopez's number. She could open them up a bit . . ."

Prince also wrote songs that tested your blackness—like "Raspberry Beret" and "Baby, I'm a Star." They were hot songs, but they just somehow made the coolest brother dance like a white dude—like Carlton on *Fresh Prince.*

You have to admit that music is becoming more and more diverse these days. I've even taken a liking to Latin music. Marc Anthony, Luis Miguel, and Ricky Martin—those boys are Latin. Their music's fun. The rap music black folks have makes you worry, it makes you fearful, it makes people want to start fighting, but when the Latin music comes on, all you want to do is have fun. Once the rhythm's got you, you start dancing uncontrollably and next thing you know, you're yelling out tribal chants and saying stuff like, "Andele, andele," and "Oh-ay, oh-ay!"

We used to have black music that made you feel good, too. It was called Motown. When you listen to Smokey Robinson, the Four Tops, or Marvin Gaye, you feel like being nice to people. You go outside and say, "How're you doing, Miss Johnson? How's everyone? How's Darryl, I mean Delicious, doing? That's good."

 **CHAPTER EIGHTEEN**

WHITE-FRIENDLY BLACKS

I really learned to appreciate the crossover. I'm not talking about a basketball move, but the ability for a black entertainer to be accepted and embraced by white folks. It's the nonthreatening approach to entertainment that gets crossover. I learned this after I starred in a Bud Lite beer commercial that ran during the Super Bowl. White people watched, they laughed, and they asked, "Who is that grown-ass man?"

It was very strange. Black folks already knew me. But being on the WB on *The Steve Harvey Show*, acting in an Eddie Murphy movie, and headlining soldout comedy tours is not the Super Bowl. You don't end the season on *The Steve Harvey Show* saying, "I'm going to Disneyland!"

The Super Bowl is different. It's the big show. It's the Academy Awards of sports. Just being on a beer commercial threw a couple logs on the fire that I called my career. It was better than a presidential pardon. And it made me white-friendly. Like Bill Cosby. Well, not that friendly. But hell, it got me thinking how different things might've been if Martin Luther King Jr.

had plugged Jell-O on a Super Bowl commercial. I love pudding and freedom. Or imagine Huey P. Newton and Eldridge Cleaver pitching Levis. White people would've loved them. You would have heard them in the checkout aisles saying, "Did you happen to catch those two Black Panthers in that Levis commercial?"

"Yeah, aren't they cute?

"Especially the one with beret."

I started thinking about how some blacks are white-friendly and others scare the crap out of even the most redneck of racists. I'm sure someplace there's a white psychologist with a theory he's willing to pontificate on the *Today* show.

"You know Katie, not every black child has to grow up as a menace to white society. Some black children can actually grow up and become white-friendly."

"How?" Katie would say.

"Katie, as numerous studies have shown, it all starts in infancy. It depends on whether the little baby goes to day care or is raised in a pool hall."

I decided to make a list of white-friendly black celebrities. My criteria is straightforward.

Number One: Would a white person freak out if they saw this particular black person approaching them at an ATM?

Number Two: Would a white person freak out if this particular black person bought a home in their neighborhood?

Number Three: ~~Would a white person freak out if this particular black person married their son or daughter?~~ (Not even Oprah is that white-friendly!)

Here's my top ten list of white-friendly black celebrities:

1. Bill Cosby
2. Oprah
3. Tina Turner
4. P-Diddy (not to be confused with Puff Daddy)
5. Whoopi Goldberg
6. Clarence Thomas
7. Cuba Gooding Jr.
8. J-Lo
9. Bryant Gumbel
10. Tiger Woods

I used the same criteria to come up with list of blacks who are the least white-friendly:

1. O. J. Simpson
2. Bill Clinton
3. Old Dirty Bastard
4. Spike Lee
5. Minister Louis Farrakhan
6. Al Sharpton
7. Ike Turner (the original Bad Boy)
8. Lil' Kim
9. Trick Daddy
10. Eminem

There are some folks who fall in the middle, like Chris Rock. Black people love him because he's funny as hell. White folks aren't quite sure because he talks about them so bad. They laugh at first, but then they don't know if they should be insulted.

Johnnie Cochran is another. White people don't trust him. He just gets too many brothers off. And they really don't like those flashy neckties. They want to know why he can't dress simply, you know, like Regis. But if they get in trouble, you know they'll be using that lifeline to call JC. And I'm not talking about Jesus Christ, but they'll be calling Johnnie like he is Jesus when they get arrested—ask Puffy.

When you're facing murder charges, you don't care nothing about the color of your lawyer or his necktie, as long as he gets your ass off.

CHAPTER NINETEEN

THE BLACK AGENDA

Black folks scored a victory when we got Black History Month. Of course it is February—the shortest month of the year. They ain't going to give us a month with thirty-one days, that's for sure. Still, I get the same thought every time Black History Month comes around: Where are all our black leaders? Where are the great individuals? Where are the legends?

We used to have leaders that led, like Martin Luther King Jr., Malcolm, Marcus Garvey, Frederick Douglass, Thurgood Marshall, Medgar Evers—people you were proud of. We had great entertainers and poets and writers like Duke Ellington, Louis Armstrong, Paul Robeson, James Baldwin, Ralph Ellison, Zora Neale Hurston, and even great business people like Madame C. J. Walker and great actors like Ossie Davis, Cicely Tyson, and James Earl Jones . . . now that is greatness.

I think most of our kids are going to think black history started with *Good Times* and *The Jeffersons*. Nobody knows anything that happened before 1972. I fear that nowadays kids sit down with their parents and say, "Daddy, tell us more about Bookman from *Good Times.*"

I'm waiting for someone to start lobbying for Gary Coleman Day. I can see Congress saying, "Yeah, that's a good idea. Gary Coleman was a cute little guy. Let's give them a half day off." That's like giving us February. Yeah, Gary Coleman Day. Why not? Let's face it. The two most famous sayings to come out of black culture are, "I have a dream" and "Whatcha talkin' 'bout, Willis?"

I can even see a Rodney King Day. We'll remember him as the man who uttered those profound words, "Can't we all get along?" He was also known for having pretty hair. He had that whole swoop thing going in the front. Remember? He looked like he was a member of the DeBarge family.

I can also see a Marion Barry Day. That'll be the day you can take off, get a hotel room, and smoke some crack. And afterward, you can go back to work and ask for a promotion or run for office or whatever it is you do.

We might even get a Johnnie Cochran Day. You can just go around to all the courthouses and get black people acquitted all day long.

You know what else is bothering me? Martin Luther King Day. I mean, what the hell is going on with that? Bit by bit, it's being transformed or truncated into just King Day. People don't even know what King they're honoring anymore.

Is it Billie Jean King Day? Are there going to be a lot of gay tennis players taking off work? Is it Rodney King Day? Every brother in a Hyundai gets whooped by a policeman? Is it Evelyn "Champagne" King Day? Everybody has to wear a sparkly dress and sing disco?

What about B. B. King Day? Everyone's got the blues? Or Burger King Day? Whoppers are ninety-nine cents?

Let's just be clear about this thing. It's Martin Luther King Day. Let's give the man his props!

The black agenda is moving along, though slowly and painfully. We won our civil rights. We got our month. We got O.J. out of jail. Next we're going after affirmative action, the end to racial profiling, and more and better opportunities in Hollywood. But I don't know if it's time for all the stuff we've been asking for—like a black president. Come on now.

If we had a black president, he or she would have to be Democrat because the Democrats love to party. Imagine the Democratic convention with a black president. You'd see the president's aide show up with chicks straight out of a video, and the president himself would get up on the podium—if they had a podium—and shout out, "Wassup, Chicago?!" He'd lead the crowd in party chants: "The roof, the roof, the roof is on fire, we don't need no water let the motherfucker burn! Burn motherfucker, burn!"

They'd get a big electric slide line going.

The convention would be off the chain. They'd be playing bid whist (six no, uptown), and people would be barbecuing and frying fish. They'd be playing dominoes in the middle of the debate. "Uh-ha, love affirmative action—fifteen!—now what was you sayin'?"

We wouldn't even need a convention hall. It would be last-minute. It would end up at the park. For the first time in history, the Democratic convention would be word-of-mouth. Everybody's meeting at the park. It started out as a regular picnic and ended up a convention. That's the thing about brothers. We don't ever plan for things like that. It just turns out to be that way.

On Election Day morning, you'd see the black presidential candidate with his posse outside the voting booths, and then we'd have Michael Buffer—the dude from all of those boxing matches—saying, "Leeeeeeeeeeeet's get ready to rum-bllllllllle!"

Really, though, it ain't time for a black president. America's not ready for that. Black folks couldn't handle it. We don't deal with stuff the same way as white folks. What's the deficit—six hundred trillion dollars or something like that? How many zeroes is that? Come on now, can you see a black president handling that kind of debt? He'd be scared to pick up the phone.

"Wh-wh-who-who is it, dawg?"

"Debt? Yeah? Six hundred trillion dollars?"

"Tell them I ain't got it, man!"

"Tell them I could put something down on it this month, but I ain't got the whole thing. I'm short.

"Will they take a postdated check or something?"

Do you think there could be a black president with all that Monica Lewinsky nonsense? Come on. We don't get fronted on like that. We can't tolerate somebody yelling our business all out in public. We don't play like that. Picture a black president having a press conference and a reporter saying, "Tell us about Monica Lewinsky."

"What?! What'd you say, playa?

"Monica?! Partna, you can't ask me that shit in front of my wife!"

Then he'd turn to his press secretary.

"Hold my jacket, dawg! This punk must think I'm Clarence Thomas!"

That's when the press conference would end. The president's aides would scatter. The Secret Service would grumble about their job, "The damn president fights too much! He's always fighting. That's why we never go nowhere with him!"

Think about this situation—Saddam Hussein with a black president. A brother doesn't deal with people two and three times about the same shit. The president would get Saddam on the phone and say something like, "I'll come over there and talk to you about it, but we only talking about this one time."

The next time they spoke and things hadn't changed, it would be, "I gotta come back over there?! Buckle up, it's gonna be me and you—mostly me—and that's all I'm sayin'!"

A brother wouldn't tolerate Saddam's nonsense. The president wouldn't even wait on the military. He'd tell the secretary of state, "I'm callin' my cousins Reggie and Bobo and Nuck Nuck. Tell them to fill up the Cadillac—it's going to be a long drive to Iraq."

We almost had a black president—Jesse Jackson. He was the closest we came. I can remember when he ran back in 1984. I voted for him and everything. I really wanted him to win. I was looking forward to those Sunday afternoon barbecues on the White House lawn. That's how we would kick it.

And I was so proud of him when he gave his speech at the convention, but I was little confused. He kept talking about "Keep Hope Alive! Keep Hope Alive!" I was wondering who the hell was Hope, and why were they trying to kill her?

I wanted to ask him, "Yo, Jesse, you need me to call up Reggie and Bobo and them and take care of that?"

Jesse was talking about running again, but he's got a lot on his mind now. He had to chill out after the story broke about his little love child with one of his assistants. Right after the scandal broke, I was telling someone how Jesse was one of my heroes. An older lady overheard my conversation and said, "I can't believe they just now catching Jesse. And everybody's acting surprised. I knew he was tomcatting around like that for years. I knew all about his *Operation Push*."

But even with all of that scandal, people pretty much left Jesse alone. Clinton had to deal with Monica Lewinsky for two years—got impeached and everything. Jesse's affair kind of slipped away, and I'll tell you why. For black folks, if you take Jesse out of the game, who we got? Al Sharpton. He's all we have left. It ain't like the bench is deep. So everybody's willing to keep quiet. We have to let Jesse slide.

But Jesse just has to try to keep himself in the game. Even with all his trouble, he still tries to stay on top of issues—like offering to go over to China and help negotiate the release of those twenty-four Navy crew members who were detained when their reconnaissance plane went down. That was real curious of Jesse. I know you wanted to get back into the political game, playa, but China?! Come on, Jesse!

Here's my Trivial Pursuit question: Were any of those twenty-four detainees black? I don't think so, which leads me to believe that Jesse didn't want to go over there to rescue nobody. I'm a grown-ass man, and there ain't but one reason why he wanted to go to China—a woman! Maybe there was more than one woman. I bet you if we went over there right now and checked, we'd find a little Kung Pow Jackson running around somewhere.

CHAPTER TWENTY

WATCH YOUR HEALTH

In the world that we live in now, you've got to be in shape. You've got to work out. I've made a plan for myself. I bought some shoes, a pair of Adidas. In a couple months, I'm going to get some sweatbands. Once I get the whole outfit together, I'm going to start working out.

But my goal is different. I'm not aiming to look like Tyson Beckford or Shamar Moore. I'm honest with myself. I've got to be. Hey, I'm a grown-ass man and I represent the big sexy—all the big, sexy players.

So I ain't trying to lose too much weight. It's like my obligation to society.

A couple of years ago, I was walking through the airport and a little boy came up to me. He was a little dude, about six or seven years old. He came up to me and said, "Ain't you Big Poppa?"

Since you can't be mean to little kids, I picked him up by his ears and said, "Hell, no! I might be a little husky, but I'll be damned if I'm notoriously B.I.G."

But I started working out on the spot. Push-ups, sit-ups,

running around the airport terminal. I felt the burn. I started burning so much, smoke detectors began going off. But I had to do something. When I got home, I even bought a Try-Bo video-tape. That's what I call it. I tried it, couldn't do it, and put that shit back on the shelf.

My shelf is full, too. It's like a library. Buns of Steel. The Ab Roller. Even the Thigh Master—and you know a brother's got to be desperate to own anything he's got to call Master.

The trouble is I'm a grown-ass man, and I ain't got time to be exercising. It makes me too tired. I got stuff to do, and I can't afford to be tired all day. Besides, I don't even like gym people. They're all happy and energetic, wearing skintight clothes and talking mess.

I was in there working out with the workout people. First off, those dudes don't need to be working out—they're already beefed up, already cut, already in damn shape. That's a problem. They're obsessive-compulsives, doing twenty, thirty reps at a time—same thing over and over. For me, once is enough. I put the weights on one-fifty, lift it, and go, "There, I did it," and I move on.

But those guys in the gym are like missionaries. They're like Jehovah's Witnesses at your front door, maybe worse. When I entered the gym, bringing in the big sexy, they immediately started telling me how to work out. Telling me what to do.

"Hey bro, you know if you really want to get in shape you do seven reps of six and you'll work your dual faburators, your tibloids, your shabbltodnots, your chuckltipilators."

The problem was that I didn't speak "gym."

"You talking about my arm, dawg? Look here, I'm a grown-ass man. If you want to talk to me about my arm, say *arm*. I ain't got time for all of that, playa."

In addition to exercise, you're also expected to eat right. Now that's tough. Being black and being on a diet doesn't mix. Black folks love to eat. We love soul food. Actually, black folks will eat any food—soul or otherwise. It ain't like we're too picky. Look, we eat stuff that needs to be boiled for eighteen hours, stuff you got to clean eighteen weeks before you cook it. Yes, I'm talking about chitterlings, also known as chitlins.

Maybe I'm not full-fledged black, because I was never a fan of chitlins. You're expected to like chitlins if you're black. At a party someone will get in your face and say, "I know you want some chitlins."

"Naw, dawg, I pass!"

I don't want to eat anything you have to clear out of the house for three days just to cook. Think about the process. After getting the chitlins, you've got to clean them for two days, soak them for a day, and then cook them for damn near twenty-four hours before you can even think about eating them. And then you've got to figure out what you're going to drench them in so you don't taste them. I don't think so. I don't even see them eating that shit on *Survivor.*

During slavery, after the master got finished with the ham, rump roast, tenderloins, getting bacon out that pig, we got what was left. And I have to give black folks credit because we made something out of nothing. We made a meal out of pig's feet, that snout, and the intestines. So much so, that if you order chitlins in a fancy restaurant today, it's going to cost you more than a filet mignon or lobster.

We ate chitlins back in the day because we had to. They were cheap. You could go to a house and have chitlins every day for two weeks—Chitlin Kabob, Chitlin Chow Mein, Chitlin Alfredo, Chitlin Helper, Chitlin Cobbler. All the grandmas would be in the kitchen saying, "I just want to use up the last of the chitlins."

"It's okay, Grandma. No more. We just had chitlins for seventeen straight days."

Then you're relieved when you get your food and don't see any chitlins on the plate, but then you see your grandma looking way too happy with herself. You know she's found a way to use them up. You know those chitlins are somewhere on your plate.

"Don't make me hurt you, Grandma? Where'd you put them?"

I'm not prejudiced against the pig. Black folks can tear a pig up. We eat pig feet, pig knuckle, pig ear. Fried pork skin? I'm on that! And what about the ham hock? I understand ham. But what the hell is a ham *hock?!* Black folks will eat everything on the pig but the oink—and that's only because we ain't learned how to cook that yet. As soon as we do, we're going to be having oink potato pie.

I know a pig sees a brother coming, and just be like, "Oh shit, there ain't gonna be nothin' left of me!"

But since we're in this era of fitness, I've been trying to eat right. But people in L.A. are on some diets that just don't make no damn sense.

"Give me a half pint of tuna, a leaf of lettuce, a strand of grass, and a small carafe of water, please." What the hell is that?!

My favorite diet is the Zone Delivery. This is where people get three special Zone meals delivered a day. It actually works. And I'll tell you why: It's expensive. After a couple of weeks, you're so poor that you can't afford to eat anything.

I've tried all the diets. I tried Slim Fast. That damn diet ain't right. A shake for breakfast and a shake for lunch? Come on, man, everybody knows a shake makes you want a cheeseburger and fries. What kind of damn diet is that? All you think about is what's missing from that meal.

I also tried to do the Jenny Craig thing for a while. Jenny Craig is the diet where you order those tiny packages of food. Hey, I'm a grown-ass man. I can't be eating meals that come in a tiny-ass package. And it costs you more than you would be spending eating out every night. Jenny Craig is a trip. You organize your entire week of meals, then you end up eating all those little bags the first day. I know I did. That first meal just ain't enough. One leads to another and then before you know it, you've eaten all those little packages . . . and you're still hungry!

I've never been as hungry as when I was on Jenny Craig. Jenny Craig ain't hungry, I guarantee you that. Her diet is so expensive. People are throwing down major money for that stuff. And Jenny's at the buffet in Vegas ordering three desserts.

Maybe white folks do well on her diet. But you won't find many black Jenny Craig success stories. To be a Jenny Craig success story, you've got to make what they call a "lifestyle change." In other words, you've got to give up eating, and as I said, we're people who like to eat. We ain't missing no meals.

I have one word to say about dieting, and it just might be the last word on the subject—Jared!

You know Jared Fogle. He's the dude who allegedly lost all that weight on the Subway diet. He's on the commercial, smiling and walking, eating Subways. He's my man. He ate Subway sandwiches and lost two hundred forty-five pounds. I was stunned when I saw that commercial for the first time.

"Hey, remember Jared?"

"Yeah. The big guy, right?"

"Look at him now. He's just eating Subway sandwiches. Look how small he is."

"That's Jared?"

"Yeah. That's him. It's the same guy."

"Shut up."

"It's for real, bro."

I love that, and you want to know why? It means one day we're going to have the Big Mac Attack Diet, the Popeye's Fried Chicken Diet, the Domino's Pizza Diet, and so on. You know they've got people working on those now. Those companies aren't going to let Subway be the only fast food place with a diet.

But health is more than diet and exercise. There are so many things you can't do nowadays that it almost takes the fun out of living. Every time you turn on the TV, you find out something new causes cancer.

The biggest culprit is smoking. Cigarettes, not weed. Weed smokers have it easy. They have it so good, it's almost like that shit is legal. You can get weed at somebody's house before you get a glass of water.

"Sorry bro, I ain't got no water. But there's a blunt in the refrigerator, though. Just go in there and help yourself."

Cigarettes are another story. I almost feel sorry for people who smoke. You've got to practically leave Earth to smoke these days. Life has changed for people who smoke at work. It used to be you could light up at your desk and blow secondhand smoke in your boss' face. That was office politics. Once they found out that secondhand smoke could kill, you'd see whole groups of smokers clustered around, trying to blow smoke under the boss' door.

Now you have to go outside to smoke a cigarette. That isn't so bad when the weather's nice. You get a pleasant five-minute break on a spring day. You catch some sunshine, check out people on the sidewalk. It's a vacation from the office. But let's say it's January eighteenth in New York. That shit ain't cute when it's cold outside, is it? You see those same people—outside like a bunch of crackheads, huddled together, shivering, sucking on their cigarettes as fast as possible. It's like speed smoking. They lean into their Bic as if it was a campfire. It's so cold they only get two puffs in before they say, "Man, I got to go back in. I'm freezing."

What's fun is watching the different styles people have when they smoke. I especially like to watch the brother who's real cool. He's the brother who's standing out front of the liquor store all day, talking shit. When he smokes a cigarette, it's a dramatization, a whole act. He gets the pack out, his arms working slow, his whole body leaning and moving almost like he's practicing tai chi. Once he gets the pack out, he taps the box like a jazz drummer. When a cigarette pops up, he turns it into a magic trick, grabbing the cigarette between two fingers, then cupping his hand around so that it disappears, and then suddenly it's in his mouth.

Then there's the cheap smoker. He's the dude who doesn't want anybody asking him for a cigarette. When he goes to smoke, he tries to hide the whole process. He's got his cigarette behind him so you can't see what he's doing. He blows the smoke behind him. Everything's a secret. Then you come over to him and he just stands there with his arm behind his back saying, "Yeah, what's up, dawg? How you doin? How you doin?"

"Cool, I'm cool, dawg. But why you got smoke coming out your ass?"

Even if you don't smoke, eat right, and exercise, there's still germs to worry about. I don't blame Michael Jackson for wearing that mask. There's some strange stuff—strange!—out there and I ain't trying to catch it.

If I do catch a cold, I take only herbal remedies. I'm scared to take cough syrup. Cough syrup makes people crazy. I don't need to get pulled over, have a cop smell my breath and ask if I'm on cough syrup. I'm not joking. In the 2000 Olympics a girl won a gold medal and had to give it back . . . they found cough syrup in her system. No joke. Cough syrup! That ain't a drug. That's embarrassing.

I heard about a man on a Southwest airplane who went crazy because he also took some cough syrup. Mike Tyson's definitely on cough syrup. He bites folks' ears off and be saying stuff like, "I'll eat your kids!" That brother's definitely on the syrup.

Know who else I bet is on that cough syrup? Bobby Brown. Actually, both Bobby and Whitney are probably sipping on some sys-zurp.

Back in the day, I used to take cough syrup all the time. If I had a really bad cough, I'd go for the Tussin—Robitussin. That's for when you had a serious cough. That stuff would knock it right out, and you could get your buzz on, too. Now I'm scared of it. I mean, you could actually use that as an excuse for why you did some old crazy stuff—like when that guy murdered someone and blamed it all on the Twinkies he'd eaten. Talk about ruining something good. After hearing that, I didn't want no trouble, so I gave up Twinkies and Hostess cupcakes, too, just in case. I kind of expect Jared to go berserk any day and blame it on Subway sandwiches.

I take these herbs now, though. I take herbs because I hate going to the doctor. You're supposed to go in for annual check-ups, but when you get to be a grown-ass man, something happens. You just feel like that ain't the move no more. The last time I went in for a physical, the doctor groaned after looking at my records.

"Well, let's see," he said. "According to your chart, the last time you were here Vanilla Ice was blowing up."

Most grown-ass men hate going to the doctor. When you were a kid and you got sick, the doctor checked your throat, looked into your ears, took your temperature. At worst, he would tell your mom to keep you out of gym for a few days. But when you're a grown-ass man and you get sick, the doctor adds one little procedure you're not prepared for. He puts on a rubber glove and asks when you last got your prostate checked.

Let me ask this, what happened in between looking in your ears and looking up your ass?

"You want to know when I last got my prostate checked? It's not like I keep track of that, you know, dawg. It's not like it's a special day."

I've never been able to answer that question. I'm not playing dumb, either. You could ask me almost any question at that moment, and I wouldn't be able to answer. When a dude's lubricating his finger so he can jam it up you-know-where, your brain goes on automatic. It goes blank. It empties out. It's spinning through thoughts like: "What the hell happened that they don't check in my throat no more?"

At least it's over quickly, and then you look at your doctor like, "How'd I do?"

If he's taking off his glove, you passed. But if he's lighting up a cigarette, that's trouble.

"Your prostate might be slightly enlarged," he said.

"Well, at least nothing else enlarged while you was checking."

Now the wife is trying to get into the business. Wives are always trying to get you to watch your health. It's like they're protecting their investment. My wife told me that I should try this thing called a colonic. I didn't know exactly what it was, but I knew the proper response, "Hey, baby, I'm a grown-ass man."

And that, she explained, was her point.

"Honey, as you get into this age group, it's going to be very important for you to know what's going on," she said. "You want to take care of yourself. You want to be healthy."

"But Boo, a colonic?!" I ask.

"I'm only asking because I love you."

At first I thought about eating a Twinkie or taking some cough syrup, but my wife was so sweet and kind and loving and well meaning that I didn't have a choice. I wasn't able to say anything except, "That makes sense, so I'll do that for you, Sweetie." A little while later, I was asking, "Okay, now what is this thing really?"

A colonic is a procedure where they force something like fourteen gallons of water straight up your ass. By the time I found that out, there was no turning back—or turning around. I was lying there, vulnerable as hell, thinking, "I'm a grown-ass man. I don't want no tubes rushing and flushing up in me."

You have to lie there and be still while the water flushes you out. I was just looking around hoping there were no cameras in that room.

So many men find themselves sick when it's too late because they won't check out what's going on. They just refuse to see the doctor. I don't completely blame them. I mean, a doctor can only check me for a hernia a couple of times and then that's it. And he better not be lighting a candle before he does it.

I know how they could get more men to go get a checkup: Get more lady doctors.

CHAPTER TWENTY-ONE

GETTING SOME

The most interesting part about sex for me is getting undressed. People are funny about getting undressed. For the most part, women prefer getting undressed in the dark. All the magazines tell them they aren't thin enough or pretty enough or whatever, basically polluting their self-confidence. Unsure about their bodies, they turn off the lights when it's that time.

"You aren't scared of the dark, are you, baby?" they ask.

"No," you say.

"Good, 'cuz I'm going to blindfold you until I get under the covers."

Men are entirely different. Guys can have a big-ass belly hanging down to their shorts, they don't give a shit. If a guy's going to get some sex, he doesn't want to waste any time trying to hide anything.

He's got no fear except that the opportunity to have sex might disappear if he doesn't act fast. So he says to himself, "I've been meaning to work out, but fuck it. And those scars? So what! My peg leg, you know, I'll just toss it over there in the corner. I've got to go for it right now!"

Just the hint of sex makes our brain cells scream, "Yes!" As we're waiting on the valet to bring our car, we're taking off our socks. We unbutton only one button—the hard one—and explain, "I'm doing this now just in case we get to your apartment and you say, 'Yeah.'"

Now, I'm a father, a husband, a motivator, a businessman, and a role model. Like every responsible grown-up man, I promote the idea that we can live out our dreams.

But the truth is something else. Only a few men—most of whom play professional basketball—get to live out their dreams, which is getting butt naked with ten women at the same time.

Seriously though, men—real men—are clear about what they want from their woman. When he's in bed with his woman—you know what I'm going to say, don't you? When a grown-ass man is in bed with his woman, he knows what he wants, he knows what he wants above all else—the remote!

We can't help it. We're men. We're physical creatures. Animals. If you ask us to do something that requires getting off the couch, we growl.

You know what you will never see? A brother in any sort of sexual dysfunction ad. Because of the myth about the black man and his sexual prowess, a brother would never admit that his equipment ain't functioning properly. Think about it, he'd be like, "Oh my God, I can't get it up, and now people are going to compare me to Bob Dole!"

I think some brothers do use Viagra, but they grind it up and mix it in their drink, and act like it's no big deal.

The thing about Viagra is you've got to know you're going to get some sex before you take it. There's nothing worse than popping one of them and then having your date go wrong. You're sitting there, and suddenly you feel a stirring down below. You look down and say, "Oh shit, that wasn't supposed to start for another hour." And you have to keep your coat on through dinner.

Then you've got some explaining to do. Either you tell your date to take a cab home because you want to sit at dinner for a while . . . alone . . . or else you admit that you made a mistake.

"I just kind of thought, you know, I was kind of overanticipating. I guess I jumped the gun on you, Babe. Popped my Viagra early. Now I don't know what I'm gonna do with this thing."

CHAPTER TWENTY-TWO

THE GLITCH

I've noticed something lately. It seems you've got to watch out for those brothers who have a little gay thing going on. I call it the glitch. A glitch in the matrix.

You've seen these dudes. They act all hard and they even look hard—like they've been pumping iron for ten years. They haven't done anything but practice how to look strong and mean. But then they do that one little thing that gives them away. The glitch.

They get real excited about Halle Berry's new hairstyle. Or a fight breaks out and the dude gets all scared and runs away, screaming in a real high-pitched voice. And you're like, "Damn, playa! What was that?!"

It's the glitch.

It's not just gays. All people have glitches. Everyone. You'll be in traffic, glance over at the car next to you, and see a guy picking his nose. Just digging real deep. He thinks because he's in his car, no one can see him. That's a glitch.

You're watching TV with a friend, and he forgets you're there and starts picking between his toenails. Nothing wrong with none of that. All of us got our glitches. Some just give you more of a jolt than others—like seeing a brother just break out and start skipping.

"Hey playa, what was with that little skip?"

Some things are hard to react to. I never know what to say. I'll be standing around a group of fellas, kicking it, just chilling and drinking a few beers. Then one of the brothers will look over and say, "Hey man, I like your outfit."

That's something another man doesn't know how to answer. Not immediately, anyway.

"What, playa? You like my outfit?!"

A man just doesn't say stuff like that to another man. You don't tell another dude you like his damn outfit. You tell a brother he's sharp. "Hey, dawg, you clean! Hey playa, hey, whoo-eeee!" But, "I like your outfit?!" That's a glitch.

"Naw, I don't think I'm going to have another beer. I'm out of here."

I have nothing against gays. I want to make that perfectly clear. But the homosexual thing has gone a little crazy now. Out in L.A., they've passed a law that says something like if you're a transvestite, you can dress up like a woman and go to work and there ain't nothing anyone can do. Your boss can't tell you to go home and change.

I ain't trying to be discriminatory, but you don't want the doorbell to ring and find it's your Federal Express guy standing out there looking like RuPaul.

"Leave the package, dawg! Just drop it and I'll get it later."

But seriously, I'm tolerant of the whole gay thing. If you want to be gay, be gay. I don't care. Ain't none of my business. But don't tell me you were born that way. They've got scientists in laboratories trying to prove that the gay thing is genetic. They're saying it's a gay gene. Do you believe that?

There ain't no damn gay gene! There are some gay guys named Gene, but don't tell me there's a gay gene.

You've got to think about this logically. If there was a gay gene, that would mean there'd be a gay gene in some if not all species that reproduce sexually. Why would it be limited only to humans? You'd have gay dogs, gay cats, gay birds, gay cows. On a farm someplace, there'd be a rooster looking at another rooster, thinking, "I'd like to cock your doodle do, Mister."

If you're gay, be gay. Have a good time. Dress up. Dance. Skip. But don't be acting like it's genetic.

What if they decide it's not a gene but a damn virus that you can catch like a cold or the flu? You come home one day, "Honey, I feel funny."

"What's the matter, baby?"

"This damn living room set is making me sick."

I'm telling you, if that starts happening, brothers will be wearing gloves and masks and lining up for the antiserum. None of them will go outside ever again.

CHAPTER TWENTY-THREE

THE WORLD TODAY

When I was coming up, we took steel to school. Yeah, we were packing. We carried it every day. But it wasn't a damn gun. It was a lunch box.

Don't get me wrong, a kid with a *Six Million Dollar Man* lunch box could be dangerous as hell, if pushed. You bust someone across the head with a *Starsky and Hutch* lunch box, it'll cause a powerful hurt. Unless it's your little gay cousin trying to swat you with his *Charlie's Angels* lunch box.

"Come on, Delicious, bring your ass on. Stop playing."

He ain't hurting no one.

But there's a lot of real violence in school today. Every time you turn on the TV, it seems like some kid has shot a teacher, shot a couple of classmates, or shot up the whole damn school. That saddens me. Little kids going crazy. That's bad.

People with kids need to be more interested in them. I think that's where we're going to start fixing the problems we got. If you've got kids, hug them. If you don't, hug somebody else's. If you know a kid, make sure they're listening to good music. Just be nice and good to them.

I'm a grown-ass man, and I don't have time to be scared of nobody who's eight years old.

Scientists need to figure it out, why does this seven-year-old boy have hostages? That's more important than looking for the gene that makes people fat. Hey, I'm a grown-ass man and I know what makes people fat—they eat too damn much! And why do we need to be putting pig's ears on a dog? And cloning sheep? Huh? Riddle me that, Batman?

I think we're researching the wrong things. Let the white coats in the lab continue looking into cures for cancer and MS and other terrible diseases, but nothing's going to be solved by telling me cigarettes are going to kill people and there's too much fat in Mexican food. I already know that.

I also know that shit happens. Sometimes you can't help but be at church when it's old folks choir. Sometimes a cop is going to pull you over because you really did run that stop sign, not because you were DWB—driving while black. Sometimes white people are going to make racist comments, and sometimes black folks will make them, too. Neither is right. Sometimes people are just stupid. We don't need scientists to prove that.

That's why I say forget trying to discover life in outer space. We need to take care of the real serious business in our world.

Listen, black folks and white folks are always going to have differences. Still, we need to understand something: We're all just folks. We got to stop the killing and the hating and learn to get along.

Dr. Martin Luther King Jr. dreamed of a day when people would not be judged by the color of their skin, but by the content of their character. That day will be near when all of us start seeing we're more alike than different. If your neighbor's air-conditioning breaks on a hot night and you don't like him, I don't believe you have to let him in your house. But I do think it's up to people everywhere, of all cultures and of every color, to be inspired by and to inspire others.

That's an important part of how I see my role as a comedian. I want to inspire people with laughter.

My wife thinks the funniest thing about me is that I make my living as a comedian, but I can get so serious about life. My daughter doesn't think it's so funny. She'll ask a simple question about her schoolwork, and I can't help but take it as an opportunity to tell her about life. I turn into a walking A&E program.

"Daddy, I can't get this math problem."

"Well, I never got math either. But don't ever let that get in your way. Honey, even if you can't figure it out, you need to have pride in yourself and what you do. Whenever you do your homework, you have to remember that your homework represents who you are and who we are as a people . . . and all of our ancestors who suffered and died so you could go to private school. Understand?"

She was eight at the time. She just wanted to know about negative numbers.

"You must not think negatively . . . WE MUST ALL COME TOGETHER AS AMERICANS!"

"Daddy, I don't feel like studying anymore."

"You don't feel like studying?!"

By this time I have covered prohibition, civil rights, and am working my way toward the Dred Scott decision when my wife takes my daughter aside and makes our stand on education simple and clear: "You know, if you're not going to work at school, you can take the G.E.D. and plan on getting yourself a paper route."

All of sudden she gets it.

"Thank you, Mommy Lorna."

You know, when I was growing up, my mother told me the same thing every day. She said, "Get your butt out of bed!" After breakfast, she'd add, "Go forth and do great things."

As I became an adult I took her seriously. I always had a plan. I started making a list of all of the great things I wanted to do: Be on TV. Star in a movie. Make lots of money. Be a good husband and father. Now I can cross writing a book off the list and get ready for the next thing. Because, as you know, I'm a grown-ass man. I got things to do.

Holla!